YOU-TURN:
Changing Direction in Midlife

ISBN: 1-4196-9501-0

ISBN-13: 9781419695018

YOU-TURN:
Changing Direction in Midlife

Over 40 Stories From People Over 40

Touch The Sun Publishing

Dr. Nancy B. Irwin

TABLE OF CONTENTS

PART 1: WHAT IS A YOU-TURN?   I
Dr. Irwin's Self-Help Tips For Blasting Through Blind Spots

PART 2: THE MIND: OWNER'S MANUAL   15
The Model of the Mind

PART 3: DETOURS, ROADBLOCKS & DEAD ENDS   23
*Change by Default: stories of unexpected changes—lay-offs,
divorce, disease, addiction, sexual discovery and more.*

Chapter 1 A Rising Star   25
*Mother of nine starts foundation for lepers in India after her
own daughter's suicide.*

Chapter 2 Heart Virtues   31
Monk is kicked out of the monastery and becomes a life coach.

Chapter 3 A Daughter's Promise   39
*Big city corporate designer leaves that life after 30 years to
take over her deceased father's small town knitting company,
saving the jobs/lives of numerous elderly employees.*

Chapter 4 Sometimes You Have to Ask God for a Sign   45
Bookkeeping business owner files bankruptcy and becomes author of 2 books on financial recovery.

Chapter 5 You Gotta Stay Strong   51
Ex-con cocaine addict/dealer turns telemarketer then real estate investor.

Chapter 6 Sometimes the Best Visions Emerge from Hard Times   61
Paralegal becomes author/speaker/visionary developer.

Chapter 7 All the Possibilities   67
Fired engineer gets fired up and becomes a published author.

Chapter 8 Hitting All the Right Notes   71
Concert pianist's remarkable recovery from partial Paralysis and spinal injuries enhances her life and career with founding of concert hall and art gallery.

Chapter 9 Why I Tell My Story   75
Paroled pedophile shares sexual offender recovery/ treatment success.

Chapter 10 What If ...?   85
Laid-off air traffic controller becomes Rabbi.

Chapter 11 The Best Laid Plans   95
Businesswoman's Lyme disease requires her constant change from one career to another.

Chapter 12 Counselor, Heal Thyself   103
Prominent attorney overcomes 20+ years of alcoholism.

Chapter 13 Never Say Never   **109**
Businessowner/conservative suburban wife/mother discovers
she is a lesbian.

Chapter 14 Pay Attention, Your Life is Calling   **113**
Crippling back injury reroutes 46-year-old woman to successful
radio talk show host.

Chapter 15 From Reel Life to Real Estate   **117**
Computer animator for one of Hollywood's most successful film
companies is laid off: starts own computer graphics business &
real estate investments.

Dr. Irwin's Self-Help Tips for When Life Blindsides You   **122**

PART 4: BACKROADS, ALTERNATE ROUTES &
TRAILBLAZING   **127**
Change by Choice: stories of self-imposed changes, born of boredom,
lack of fulfillment and other internal forces.

Chapter 16 The Good News Garage   **129**
Culinary institute catering director starts non-profit rehabbing
used cars for low-income people.

Chapter 17 Dream Weaver   **135**
Vegetarian cooking instructor/mother becomes successful
fashion designer.

Chapter 18 Healing Energies   **139**
Harvard lawyer/UCLA Law professor becomes holistic healer.

Chapter 19 Finding the Way Out   **147**
Emotionally abused wife leaves her husband with 2 small
children in tow.

Chapter 20 From Critic to Medic   **153**
PhD theatre critic goes to med school at age 40.

Chapter 21 Learn to Believe   **157**
Pioneer in the learning disabilities education field veers off the mainstream.

Chapter 22 Synchronicity   **163**
Cable talk show host moves to North Dakota and revives vintage movie theatre.

Chapter 23 You Can Fly   **167**
Flight from Corporate America to solo entrepreneur.

Chapter 24 Living with Passion   **171**
50ish divorcee seeks out high school sweetheart and becomes relationship coach.

Chapter 25 Learn to Change   **179**
Medical tech turned actress becomes a school teacher.

Chapter 26 The Repair Pro   **183**
Handyman fixes himself by leaving company and starting own business at age 47.

Chapter 27 Life is Short   **187**
79-year-old singer/business owner goes to law school.

Chapter 28 Two Steps Back, Three Steps Forward   **193**
Clothing industry numbers-crunchers becomes applied psychologist.

Chapter 29 Follow Your Bliss   199
*Twice divorced mother of 3 enters seminary at age 47, ordained
as Presbyterian minister at age 52.*

Chapter 30 The Theory of the Cosmic Slingshot   203
Jet setting photojournalist becomes public diplomat.

Chapter 31 Kick Your Doubts in the Teeth   209
LA Times reporter turns into a web designer.

Chapter 32 Never Too Late   213
*80-year-old grandmother leaves abusive husband after 47 years of
marriage, founds domestic abuse website.*

Chapter 33 Just Getting Started   217
*Executive sales director and father leaves security at age 45 to start
own marketing business.*

Chapter 34 Aleikum salaam wa rahmat Allah wa karakatu   221
Unhappy wife/businessowner moves to Egypt to discover herself.

Chapter 35 A Little Music, A Lot of Love   229
*Musician leaves life on the road when he learns his son is
autistic; becomes therapist for special needs children.*

Chapter 36 Escaping the Desk   235
Bored office worker becomes a real estate agent.

Chapter 37 Man on Fire   239
*A fire in his car becomes fire in his belly...Texas sales
account executive becomes successful Hollywood actor.*

Chapter 38 The Best Years 245
Laid-off contractor starts own business at age 44.

**Chapter 39 Find the Goal Posts and Keep Aiming
for Them** 247
*Technologist for mutual fund company becomes "think tanker"
for counterinsurgency and counterterrorism.*

Chapter 40 Love is Our Spiritual Glue 253
*Housewife/mother goes to college at age 60, finishes doctorate
at age 70.*

Chapter 41 The Sound of Success 259
*Single retail music store owner becomes husband/father/
representative for distributors at age 42.*

Chapter 42 Click! 263
Advertising writer becomes comedic cabaret singer/author.

Chapter 43 Find Your Passion and Live with It 269
Advertising writer becomes comedic cabaret singer/author.

Dr. Irwin's Self-Help Tips for Veering Off on Your Own 274

**Dr. Irwin's Self-Help Tips for Entrepreneurs: Driving
Your Business on a Shoestring Budget** 275

PART I: WHAT IS A YOU-TURN?

WHAT IS IT WITH society and numbers? Start school at age 6, graduate high school at 18, finish college by 22 and retire at 65. And who says we have to stop growing, changing and evolving as we continue to grow up? Not me. And not the millions who, as they reach what I call "middlescence," stand at the crossroads of their past and future and decide to take an alternate route.

It's easy to get on the wrong path or get sidetracked, or even get run off the road. Maybe you reluctantly agreed to follow in your father's footsteps and become a doctor, or you had dreams of being a writer until an English teacher scoffed at your talents. And now here you are, eager for new challenges or revisiting old ones, yet you find yourself stalled with excuses. "Can't teach an old dog new tricks." "I'm too old to start over." "It's too late." "Oh, I could never do that." "I've been doing this for so long, why quit now?"

It's like driving 50 miles out of your way. Frustrating, isn't it? But do you just give up and say, "Oh, well, I'll just keep driving down the wrong road"? Of course not! You'd turn around, wouldn't you? So why stay on the same course of life or career? Maybe school, family or unforeseen circumstances mapped out your life and set you down that road. But now you're looking for a new direction and new meaning.

You're not alone. You're one of the 84 million born in the United States between 1946 and 1964 who have now reached middle age and are on a quest to find a new way of life. By our very existence, we changed the economy, music, medicine, fashion, technology—you name it, we did it! So don't stop now! The only limits are the ones we place on ourselves.

Some plunge headlong into midlife crises, but there is nothing critical about midlife! Instead, believe in the transformative powers of middle age. This is the time to turn it all around, to please yourself, to make your own choices and to create what you want. All you need is a "you-turn."

A U-turn is when a vehicle goes 180 degrees into the opposite direction of its previous path. Likewise, a you-turn, as I like to call it, is a complete reversal in opinion, action or policy. When you embrace a you-turn into your life, you set in motion a self-fulfilling prophecy of empowerment and possibilities.

My life journey took me on many detours until I made my own you-turn.

I'm not an exceptional person—my SAT scores were pretty low, and I was always the last kid picked for any team sport. (Not only was I not chosen; they generally called the game off completely!) Originally from Atlanta, Georgia, I trained to be an opera singer. My passion for performing led me to New York City, where I changed direction and began a career as a stand-up comic. I worked gigs all over the country and internationally. I moved to Los Angeles in 1994, when I heard Hollywood needed more blondes. While I was doing fairly well as staff emcee at the Melrose Improv, comics only work about 30 minutes a day, so I had a lot of time on my hands. I began volunteering in the community, a move that would induce my biggest life change to date. While working for Children of the Night, a shelter for sexually abused children, I experienced an epiphany—I wanted to spend my life educating, counseling and advocating for kids like this. Not only did this experience wake up the healer in me, but it allowed me to begin healing the wounds from my own childhood sexual abuse at the hands of a clergyman. I decided to pursue a doctorate in psychology, specializing in the prevention and healing of child sexual abuse. Even with a you-turn of this magnitude, I continue to push the envelope. For example, I now am training to treat molesters, which keeps me standing in the empowering position of compassion rather than victimization. Further, treating perpetrators is the best way to help victims.

Today, in addition to my thriving private therapy practice in Los Angeles, I'm a busy public speaker for Children of the Night, as well as for other advocate groups like Planned Parenthood and the Rape, Abuse, and Incest National Network (RAINN). I'm a member of the California Psychological Association, the Southern California Society of Clinical Hypnosis and the American Academy of Experts in Traumatic Stress, and I sit on the Education Committee of the California Coalition on Sexual Offending. Ironically, I've appeared on more radio and TV shows as a therapist than I ever did as a comedian!

I once thought my entire first and second careers were a misstep, or that I was just idling, wasting time. But my 10 years in opera and nine in comedy were not mistakes; a significant portion of my patients are creative artists—how could I truly understand them had I not been a part of that world? I believe that life is a dynamic process and everything happens for a reason. I knew somewhere deep inside, there was a purpose. If I hadn't been a bored comedian, I may never have sought out volunteer work and had the healer in me awakened. If it weren't for that "mistake," I'd never be where I am now.

Mistakes get a bad rap, but they are merely stepping-stones to success. I defy you to find a successful person who never made a mistake or acted without fear. We are geared to think that mistakes are the worst possible outcome, as if someone's keeping score or we collect them next to our name like demerits as evidence of failure. Like the longer your list of mistakes, the bigger a loser you are. But mistakes are valuable learning tools, pushing the envelope toward your success. Winners lose all the time. So embrace your mistakes and learn from them!

One of the first things I have my "mistakaphobic" clients do is to deliberately make a blunder. Go ahead and try it. This exercise gives you permission to fail and frees you to take risks. If you aren't making mistakes, you aren't living. (That said, your practice mistakes should never be ones that would intentionally harm another person or yourself.) Pick an activity you KNOW you'll fail and do it. What's the worst that can happen? Will you fall off the earth? Of course not! You might be surprised at what you discover ... that you underestimated yourself, or that you have an untapped talent or two. For example, if you think you are a sucky singer, go to a karaoke night. You'll dissolve the block of fear and learn to truly value your strong suits and skills.

If you want to make a change, mistakes and all, you've come to the right place. This isn't a how-to book—it's a can-do collection of proof that ordinary people can do great things. It contains thought-provoking, energizing and refreshing stories from men and women who wanted to change their lives and did. Some knew what they wanted, others didn't. No one made his or her you-turn exactly the same way. But they were just like you—they felt trapped, stuck and bored, and that's a great place to start. At least you know how you feel. Many people are so steeped in their denial that they are completely desensitized to pain. But pain is GOOD! It is a signpost and signal that you're going in the wrong direction. Here's your opportunity to correct it and get going in another direction. Winners use pain as an alarm clock that something's not working and make adjustments. Losers use pain as proof that they are failures.

Let's get started making your own you-turn toward a new life. Don't feel overwhelmed, we'll go in baby steps.

Begin by asking yourself the following questions to get in gear, and let them sink in before answering. I would suggest answering one at a time, preferably before bed. Make each one an essay—write down every thought, feeling and impulse (positive and negative) you have for that answer. Then put it away until you've completed them all.

1. What would you do if you knew you could not fail?

2. If money were no object, what would you be doing?

3. If time were no obstacle, what would you be doing?

4. If you were given six months to live, how would you spend them? What would you want to say, and to whom, on your deathbed?

5. If you could be present at your own funeral, what would you want to hear the eulogizers saying about you?

6. When you are 100 years old and sitting on your porch talking to your great-great-grandchildren, what do you want to share with them about your life? What would you like to look back on and see that you did— what you stood for, what you had to say?

7. If you had time to volunteer in the community, what would that look like? Would you read to the blind, save the whales, clean up the environment, serve in a soup kitchen, visit terminal kids in a hospital? What causes could you take a stand for? How could you help to make the world a better place? A great way to begin this exercise is to ask yourself what angers/bothers/upsets you most about the world? How can you help change that?

8. What are your strengths and limitations? Write down all the things that are working in your life, followed by those you'd like to change.

9. Which is scarier: change, or staying bored and miserable where you are?

10. What is the worst possible outcome you can imagine? Could you survive if that ensued?

That took a lot of work, I know. Are you any closer to what it is you'd like to do? Any changes you'd like to make? Don't have a clue? No problem. There are ways to jumpstart your life changes.

Want some more?

1. Think back when you were a kid. Who/what did you want to be when you grew up? Write them ALL down...discount nothing... don't judge yourself. You identified with that person/s for a reason.

2. What are your five favorite movies ever? Five favorite books? You identify with the message or the characters in some way. Explore that common denominator. It is an integral part of YOU.

3. What are your most important values?

4. What are the happiest, most fulfilling, or most outstanding peak moments in your life thus far?

5. What are you most proud of?

6. What are you good at? Make a list of all those things you like to do, and those that you are really good at (they may or may not intersect).

7. Take a survey of five diverse people (professional, friend, neighbor, family member, etc.) and ask them what they see as your three greatest strengths, as well as three areas that could use improvement.

8. What three adjectives would those closest to you use to describe you?

9. What do people come to you for? What sort of help or advice?

10. If you could wave that proverbial magic wand, what would you suddenly have/be/do?

"Use what talent you possess.
The woods would be very silent if no birds sang
except those that sang best."

Henry Van Dyke

Self-Help Tips to Blast through Blind Spots

1. Don't wait until you aren't scared. You'll be dead. Most of us are scared all the time! Change does not require fearlessness, but it does require courage. Courage is not being fearless—it's doing what is right in the face of fear. Without fear, there'd be no courage.

2. Realize that it's much scarier to stay where you are than to go for your goal. Anticipation is generally scarier than reality.

3. Late bloomers smell just as sweet as early or on-time bloomers. In fact, the latter may all be dead and you come out smelling like a rose. Trust your own bud to blossom in its own time.

4. Afraid of making a mistake? Well, what are you in the midst of right now? Continuing down a path that is no longer fulfilling for you is compounding your pain. If you take a risk and it doesn't work out,

then at worst, you'll have made two mistakes instead of one. So keep making mistakes until you get it right.

5. Volunteer in your community. We are born to serve, give, teach, heal, enlighten. If you go out into the community and give something of yourself, you'll awaken something inside of you—guaranteed. We all have many facets and gifts. They can be sparked anytime, anywhere, and generally light up very quickly when we are selflessly involved. Your untapped talents will rise to the surface when you work with the developmentally challenged, help with a political campaign, deliver food to AIDS patients, collect recyclables—the list is endless. Selfless service can alter your life.

6. No "shoulds" allowed! Many people torture themselves with "I *should* have X by now!" or "I *should* have done X by now!" or "I *should* be X by now!" As the late, great psychologist Dr. Albert Ellis said, "Stop should-ing all over yourself!" He also said, "Stop must-urbating!" for those haunted with "I *must* have X" or "I *must* be X" or "I *must* get X." Replace *should* and *must* with "choose to," and see how many possibilities open up to you—e.g. "I chose to be a stand-up for nine years." This allows you to take responsibility for your actions and frees you to make a new choice.

7. Most skills are transferable. If you choose to view life from a linear perspective, it would appear that my decade each in opera and comedy were wasted. However, viewing it dynamically, we see how it led to my new career. Trust me, the road from stand-up comedy to mental health is a very short one. My stagecraft enabled me to add humor to the austere; it prepared me for public speaking, working with creative artists in Hollywood, and for writing this book! Make a list of all your skills. Then list what you like to do on your days off. Let those two lists marinate for a few days, then start connecting the dots. And don't limit yourself to something that already exists … create your own niche.

8. Many people do know what they'd rather be doing but are simply afraid to make the change. Start by simply making a list of all the

steps of action that would be required if you had the courage to proceed. Review your list daily. Next, pick a date when you'd ideally like to attain the goal. Work backward and plan each step toward that goal at a reasonable working pace for you. This allows you to be psychologically geared and excited about the whole process, rather than overwhelmed. Perhaps the first simple, baby step is just looking up one phone number of a contact. For the following step, write out a script of what you'd like to say to that contact when you reach him or her. Don't make the call yet; just write the script. Make the call when it is in your plan to take that action step.

9. Many people don't have a clue what their right path is. They just know they are in pain or unfulfilled now. Well, your imagination is a magic wand. If you feel stuck, just ask yourself: "If I were to imagine that I DID know what I wanted to do with my life, it would be X." Give yourself time to realize the answer. Remember that YOU are the magic wand ... the agent for change.

10. It really doesn't matter *what* you do. It's *who* you are while you're doing any and everything you do. So we really all have the same purpose. To think that there is *one* thing you are "supposed" to do is placing enormous, undue pressure on yourself.

Anyone can do this. Just set a goal, lay out the steps that you need to take—remembering to take one step at a time—and always be sure to celebrate the successes you create along the way. Keep supportive people around you.

Don't wait for the fears and doubts to disappear—they never will. Because you are human. Take action in spite of the fears. We are all scared and doubtful every day of our lives—relationships, family, finances, work, it's never-ending. But you can soft pedal those feelings rather than letting them run you over.

The people who were kind enough to contribute to this book discovered their own you-turns, and many made their own mistakes. As you read their stories, you'll notice that the same words pop up:

fear, anxiety, unknown, belief, failure and success. Each of these people faced, faltered, fell and got back up again to fulfill their destinies. Some changed by default—life or other people forced them to change—and some chose it on their own. Embracing their inner power to change their lives, they all turned their middle-age burnout into a middle-age blaze. You can, too.

"How old would you be if you didn't' know how old you were?"

Satchel Paige

PART 2

THE MIND:
OWNER'S MANUAL

"It is not the strongest of the species that survive, nor the most intelligent, but the most responsive to change."

Charles Darwin

PART 2
THE MIND: OWNER'S MANUAL

W E ARE ALL BORN with a mind, and most people don't have a clue how it works. I'm going to give you the Manual for the Mind so you can start driving your life in the direction you choose, rather than staying on a dead-end street.

At birth, the mind is like a blank slate. (The ole Tabula Rasa theory, for those of you who have studied psychology.) My belief is that we are all born to win. We're filled with joyful, positive, loving energy at birth— when you smile at the average child, she usually smiles back, right? Arguably, our ability to fail, to sabotage, to be violent, etc., is learned— and whatever we learn, we can un-learn. We're hard-wired to attain our goals so we can procreate and make our species go on. We've been this way since we were cavemen, and it's safe to assume we always will be. To that end, we are innately equipped with a powerful survival mechanism called "fight-flight response." Our primitive ancestors would go into fight-flight mode if they heard a saber-toothed tiger growling around outside the cave. In a heartbeat, they'd either grab a spear and fight the danger, or flee to the back of the cave. Modern man does the same thing. If you were held up at gunpoint, you'd make the instantaneous decision to kick the perpetrator's butt (fight) or run like heck (flight). Modern man also has a psychological parallel to fight-flight: anxiety and depression. Anxiety is an attempt to fight future danger or control the uncontrollable (borrowing pain from the future). Depression (hanging on to pain from the past) is an attempt to flee danger by retreating into our own private cave through isolation, or numbing our emotions through drugs, alcohol, cigarettes, gambling, sex, shopping, you name it. But underlying all these options—fight, flight, anxiety, depression—is a positive intent. We never do anything to deliberately hurt ourselves or one another, though it certainly can appear that way. Even serial killers (and I'm not defending them!) are trying to feel powerful and in control.

The second you exit the womb, you start filling up the endless hard drive of your mind known as the subconscious. From infancy throughout adolescence, we are constantly plugging bits of data into this database and filing it away for future reference. This includes both positive and negative experiences, which become points of reference by which we measure all incoming data. These differ with our various experiences, personality traits, cultures, etc., but they are "known facts" that prompt our responses. For example, let's say in first grade you sit behind a boy named Zach who always steals your lunch. You'd file away a "fact" in the form of a negative association with boys named Zach, and to protect you in the future, you create a bias toward anyone named Zach. If he had red curly hair, you might create another bias toward boys with curly red hair. Adults don't fare much better. Let's say I wear a green blouse to a sushi bar to meet my boyfriend for dinner one night, and he dumps me. How likely will I be to wear that green blouse again? To dine at that sushi bar? I more than likely would create negative associations with these, even though my intelligence tells me neither is to blame for the break-up! But as we have already established, intelligence and behavior have nothing to do with one another. Scientifically, I go into fight-flight mode when I am dumped. Brilliantly designed, this protective device goes to work to stave off future danger of a similar nature. From "avoid the saber-toothed tiger" to "don't wear that green blouse," we remain strongly wired to survive. By acknowledging our mindset, we can neutralize those negative associations and be free.

We address our fears through positive associations as well. This is how superstitions were born. Holding a rabbit's foot is good luck, breaking a mirror is bad luck. My favorite example: when the phenomenal tenor Luciano Pavarotti was waiting to begin one of his earliest opera performances, he twirled a bent nail in his hand as he nervously paced backstage. When his cue was called, he absentmindedly took the nail with him and subsequently had to shove that hand in his pocket, leaving the nail there through the whole opera. Of course, Pavarotti received thunderous applause and a standing ovation, after which he proclaimed "This is my lucky nail!" He allegedly never went onstage again without that bent nail in his pocket. Now I ask you, did Pavarotti's glorious talent come from a nail? Of course not! But he made a positive association in his subconscious mind that night, and part of him believed he was safe and secure as long as he had his lucky nail.

As children, we are pure subconscious material—little sponges taking in and believing everything we are told. Santa Claus. The Tooth Fairy. The Boogeyman. Children cannot judge information, so they just believe. They are pure hypnosis. So if a child is told, especially by someone they trust, "You are stupid" or "You'll never amount to anything ... you're just like your father," the child will file away this "fact" in his subconscious. It may be painful, but it can become a self-fulfilling prophecy. (We have a natural tendency, as you may have noticed, to believe the negative stuff more than the positive. Why? Simple explanation: because back in the jungle, only the "bad" stuff could hurt us. *Much* more vital information.) Conversely, for lucky children who grow up hearing "You are beautiful" and "You are smart," that too can become a self-fulfilling prophecy. The good news is that *none* of these is a true fact. They are *beliefs*. And we can always change our beliefs, can't we? Of course we store data regarding gravity and biology, but most of our daily existence is predicated on our belief systems. Law, religion, education, psychology ... these are all belief systems that can empower you—or not. It's always your choice. Children are the victims of the beliefs of those in their environment; however, as an adult with the power of choice, you can always change your beliefs, and hence your behavior. Our beliefs drive our behavior, and all behavior comes from subconscious programming—that stuff that started growing the moment we entered the world. Therefore, to change our behavior, we first must change our beliefs. In order to effect positive change more easily, it helps to uncover the underlying need. On a primitive level, human beings hate change because we can only operate from the information we already know ... all those positives and negatives that are filed in our database. If no known is there, we avoid it, because in the jungle what's new or different might kill us. That being said, we are enormously capable of changing in the blink of an eye. It is quite easy to add new positive beliefs to our database, with our conscious mind's permission and choice. Our Neanderthal predecessors really couldn't do that. They had other priorities. Modern man, however, can override a previous default setting in an instant.

Around ages 8-12, we grow a filter of judgment and are able to assess incoming information rather than blindly accepting everything as truth. This gives birth to the conscious mind, which houses all our intellectual skills: logic, reasoning, decision-making skills and willpower. The reason most of us fail or lose or sabotage is that the conscious mind (which is where we keep our intelligence!) is only about 12% of all our mental capabilities. That means a whopping 88% comes from the subconscious, which is where we get our behavior. This is why bright people keep doing stupid things over and over and over again. They "know" better, but keep getting pulled into the old negative pattern. Luckily, this massive storehouse of power known as the subconscious is easily manipulated by our conscious mind. Even better, we can align both these storehouses so that we have 100% of our power supporting us in attaining our goals. Think of it like this: the subconscious is a machine, just like your car. Your car is a much more powerful physical entity than your body, but how do you get anywhere in that car? You, the driver, guide it. Just as your car doesn't care whether you turn right or left, the subconscious mind doesn't care if you are a smoker or a non-smoker, if you love your job or despise it, if you are obese or at your ideal weight. The subconscious is extremely obedient and indiscriminately follows any order it is given. Knowing this now, you have a choice: you can consciously drive your life or continue to be unconsciously driven by old patterns.

Your car takes its commands from a driver, who physically steers the car in the desired direction. The subconscious, however, takes its commands from the conscious mind through words, images and symbols. We attract whatever we focus on, and whatever we focus on expands. That, of course, can be good or bad. Sadly, most people live in a world of "Oh, it's hard to quit smoking," "Every time I lose weight, I gain it right back," "I'm too old to get married" or "Life has passed me by." Your constant thoughts and statements are self-hypnotic suggestions that create your reality. For that reason, you must focus on what you *do* want, not on what you *don't* want—because your subconscious can't tell the difference between what you truly want and what you say. It processes information very literally and simply, like a child. You probably know that you don't tell a child what *not* to do, right? Yet most parents tell their children "Bobby, stop slamming that door!" "Don't hit your sister!" "Don't put those beans up your nose!" Guess what they do? You guessed it—slam, hit, beans up the nose. Those action words and powerful images are instantly programmed into Bobby's mind and consequently into his behavior. Simply rewording your commands to Bobby could completely change his behavior: "Thank you for closing the door gently." "I love it when you get along well with your sister." "I need you to keep the beans on the plate."

Adults' minds work pretty much the same way. Focusing on *not* doing something is simply drawing attention to it. When you're driving on the highway, you don't focus on what you don't want, do you? "OK, don't hit that red car. Don't hit that bus. Really don't hit that police car!" What would happen? You want to focus on driving safely, defensively, intuitively, and getting to your destination safely. Change your language; change your life. Start focusing on attracting your ideal job, not getting out of this crappy one. Start focusing on the many ways you *can* improve your life, rather than all the reasons why you can't. Focus on how exciting change can be rather than how scary. Focus on creating a fulfilling intimate relationship rather than how there are no quality people out there. This is beyond positive thinking: it's the Law of Attraction. Coupled with the law of action, you'll be amazed at how quickly the power of your mind will begin drawing those things into you. You know it works because it has always worked in a negative way. I invite you to turn it all around now.

MODEL OF THE MIND

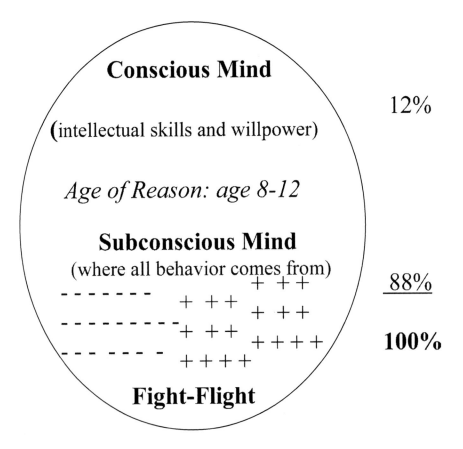

Conscious Mind

12%

(intellectual skills and willpower)

Age of Reason: age 8-12

Subconscious Mind
(where all behavior comes from)

88%

100%

Fight-Flight

PART 3

DETOURS, ROADBLOCKS & DEAD ENDS

"The ultimate measure of a man is not where he stands in moments of comfort and convenience, but where he stands at times of challenge and controversy."

Reverend Martin Luther King, Jr.

Chapter 1

A RISING STAR

---

*"The things 1 was concerned about before, 1 realized were
really ridiculous. My problems, my outlook and perspective
have changed. 1 don't see things the way 1 once did—how can
anyone see things the same way after what 1've seen?"*
– Becky Douglas, "Breaking the Curse"

By Becky Douglas & Nancy 1rwin

IN 2000, MY HUSBAND and I received the phone call that every parent
dreads. Our beautiful daughter, Amber, after a lifetime of suffering
from bipolar disorder, had committed suicide at the age of 24. Her
dad and I and her siblings, all eight of them, mourned the loss of such a
wonderful, giving soul.

She was in college at the time of her death, and when we went to collect her things we discovered that she had been sending part of the money that we sent her each month to India to support an orphan there. When arrangements for her funeral were being made, we asked people to donate to the orphanage in her name, in lieu of flowers.

The outpouring was so tremendous that the orphanage asked me to be on the board of directors. I decided that if I was going to commit, I had better go and see what it was all about. So in 2001, I found myself flying to India. Upon first glance, the orphanage, by U.S. standards was extremely poor—the children ate and slept on the floor—but by Indian standards they had more than enough.

Then one day, coming back to the orphanage from my hotel, I came face to face with human suffering so intense that I felt like I was drowning and gasping for air. Every time the car stopped, beggars would surround us and many of them didn't have limbs; the majority had festering sores covering their bodies and a few of these people had their small children with them. We don't see that in America. We don't see people living with gangrene, putting their hands that are rotting away, up to your window begging for money.

I just wanted to close my eyes.

But a young woman crawled up to our car and I watched her as she scratched at the car's tire. She looked up and her dark eyes seemed to pierce right through me. That's the first time I really felt connected, and I knew that I had to do something for her.

I learned that the beggars with the disfigured arms and legs had leprosy, a contagious skin disease, that causes serious and permanent damage to the body, including paralysis, gangrene, and deformation. It frequently results in the loss of fingers, nose, and limbs. I was ignorant, I'm embarrassed to say, but I thought leprosy had been eradicated from the planet, that it was just a word from the Bible.

I was astonished to discover that not only does leprosy still exist, but so do leprosy colonies. I learned that 70% of the world's leprosy cases are in India and that the patients must move into leprosy colonies because their families disown them. More upsetting than the disfiguring effects of leprosy was the fact that in India, leprosy is not thought as a disease, but rather, as a curse from God, making it something a person deserves.

When someone has leprosy, they're shunned by their community, family and friends. The beggars had not only lost their limbs, but their homes, their jobs, their families and any hope for a future. So I wasn't just battling the disease; I was battling the prejudice that runs deep in Indian society. Not only did I come up against resistance within the community and those in the medical profession, but also even with those infected with the disease. These people are treated almost like criminals. I couldn't find any local medical community program to help; in fact, most medical clinics and hospitals in the area even refused to extend care to the leprosy patients.

When I came back to my comfortable home in Peachtree Corners, Georgia, the image that kept running through my mind, coming to me in the middle of the night was that young woman who was begging me for help—who needed *my* help.

But who was I to help anyone a continent away? I was a middle-aged suburban housewife with eight kids. And I certainly didn't know anything about putting together a public service organization in southeastern India! Yet that woman's eyes haunted me. So I called four close friends, and we sat around my kitchen table and discussed various ideas and solutions. Together, we formed Rising Star Outreach in March 2002, became incorporated, and received our 501(c)(3) tax-free status.

My hometown newspaper, *The Atlanta Journal-Constitution*, wrote a story about Rising Star's efforts. Soon we started getting even more help from people and businesses, including Marriott, the national and international hotel chain. With all this attention, we started raising money for food, shelter and medicine.

I went back to India with a group of medical students hoping to provide care to the people I had met in the leprosy colony. I made up my mind that I would look at them when I went in because that was the one thing I had not been able to do when I first saw them on the street. I thought, "I've come all this way, I'm going to look at them" and I thought if I could just look into their eyes I could do fine.

Many of the leprosy-affected people in the colonies had children. Since leprosy has a genetic component, the children were the most likely people to contract the disease. I had to think of something to help them. Through donations to Rising Star, the first official Rising Star Outreach children's home was opened in April of 2004. We took in 27 children from the leprosy colonies.

By 2005, a second children's home opened for 32 additional colony kids. Now officially recognized by the Indian government, Rising Star has been commended for the high standard of care and excellence maintained in the school as the children prepare to enter mainstream society.

In October of 2006, construction began on a permanent school for the children. The 13 acre property will also house a children's village, comprised of several homes for children in which the children will live until the age of 18. It will also have schools from pre-school up through the twelfth grade.

While Rising Star was happy to have finally found a way to successfully care for the children of leprosy victims, the suffering of their families who remained behind in the colonies could not be ignored— the parents were still out begging in the streets. No matter how much money and medicine I gave them there was no end in sight. I had to think of a way for them to help themselves without begging.

Then Padma Venkatraman, former UN representative and daughter of the former president of India, stepped in. She said that throwing money at the poor is part of the problem; they had to learn how to sustain themselves—they had to go to work.

Work? How? Many of these people had no limbs or were so despondent, not to mention disabled, that they couldn't get up out of the dirt. But Padma convinced me that what they needed was a small business loan. I know what you're thinking—in America, a bank would give a $100,000 or a loan or more so a person could start a marketing design firm, a car dealership, a stationery store or a repair shop. Our loans were small by U.S. standards (usually around $15-20 U.S. dollars), but they enabled the patients to purchase equipment and supplies necessary to begin their own small business, whether it was for a turkey or for carpenter's tools.

Through Padma's program, for the first time in known history, those afflicted with leprosy were provided with a practical alternative to begging and were rising above the stigma of their disease. We now have about 1000 residents in more than 40 leprosy colonies with their own small businesses. Some of them even have employees!

Now our mission is to help the leprosy colonies in Southern India become thriving, self-sufficient communities by the year 2020. We've come a long way since my kitchen table. We're now building a complex, near Chennai, India, which will include two boarding hostels that can house about 300 boys and girls, and a school that will eventually hold about 800. The children will be attending the school and living in the hostels away from their families. Leprosy is genetic, so in order to stop the cycle, the children must live and study at the center. Classes are taught in their native language but emphasize proficiency in English. The rest of the curriculum is comparable to the best public schools in India.

Rising Star has four paid employees in America, whose salaries are paid with donations from board members. Everyone else is a volunteer. One hundred percent of all the other donations go to aid programs. Rising Star's operating budget is about $750,000 a year. I'm proud to say that Rising Star also funds a mobile medical clinic for the leprosy patients and their families.

In 2007 Rising Star became the subject of a 2007 documentary, *Breaking the Curse*, produced by Kos Films and narrated by former CNN anchor Daryn Kagan. Now our efforts are receiving wide-scale attention.

I wanted to make a difference, and I needed to make my daughter's life and death mean something. I didn't know what to do or where to go, but it was as if a pair of unseen hands had taken me by my shoulders and nudged me along this path. This is where I ended up—helping the leprosy-afflicted and their families. It's been a bittersweet journey, and I've certainly felt loss and victory, but I've learned that every dark day has sunlight and every sky at twilight has its rising star.

Chapter 2

HEART VIRTUES

"Are you ready to give up all hope of having a better past?"

– Greg Mooers

By Greg Mooers & Nancy Irwin

THE THREE GREATEST HUMAN regrets for people on their deathbed are ...

1. I wish I had spent more time in contemplation
2. I wish I had taken more risks
3. I wish I had left something of lasting value behind

In other words, get in there, live life. Now. One of my mentors once said, "What would you dream if you knew you couldn't fail?" I've had many dreams and feel fortunate and blessed that I took the steps that I did to achieve those dreams and sit here now sharing my story with you.

I'm the founder and president of LifeCamp. Through my workshops, consulting services and coaching, I empower the hero that lives inside us all to become the master of our career and our relationships. That's a quick little summation of the path I'm on now, but it took many years and starts and stops to get here.

When I was 18, I was really tough to be around. I was always challenging people—what truth was, what their belief systems were. I would challenge everything to see if it was real, especially religions and relatives. But one day I noticed my mother was actually changing. She gave me a book of what she was involved in, called *Sayings of Yogananda*, the founder of the Self-Realization Fellowship. I remember sitting down with the book and thinking, "I'm just going to slice this to pieces. It's just another belief system with holes in it." I read that book cover to cover, and by the time I was done, I said, "Well, there is not a single thing in this book I disagree with. This must be my path." But I didn't do anything about it; I just went back to my fraternity and my typical college life.

Then, around 21, after I'd graduated from college, I got a job in sales at Intel. At first it was a lot of fun, and I made a lot of money—but I felt empty. A few years later, at 27, I woke up at 2 in the morning, crying and pleading, "Lord, either give me something to live for or take my life, because there's got to be more to life than this." This was the first of my many midlife crises.

A week later, I was on the phone with a friend when he suddenly remarked, "You know, you've got potential but you're not very happy. What do you really want to do?" I told him that I wanted to improve efficiency for people; I wanted to write artificial-intelligence software for large corporations. He came right out and said, "Well, I'll be your partner; I'll finance your company. You can stay with me until you find a place to live and I'll mentor you." And I was like, "Done!" Two weeks later, I gave my notice and moved from New Jersey to Dallas, Texas.

So there I was in Dallas starting a new company. But after I'd hired my fifth employee, I hit another wall. I remember looking at a building and thinking with dread, "You know, *that's* where I'm headed." And this little voice popped up and said, "But that's not what you want." Well, what *did* I want? That little voice answered, "I want to know my soul." It was like an instant replay of when I was a teenager, reading *Sayings by Yogananda*. Through the years, actually, I had taken a few classes on meditation and had started praying every day because I was seeking *something*. I wasn't sure what it was, but I knew that it was not outside me, it was inside me. So I signed up for an inside-out process of empowerment. I gave my company to my employees and moved to Escondido, California, to be a monk.

For eight years, I meditated 5-6 hours per day, practicing silence and studying the lives of heroes as a pet project. The more I learned about these independent masters, the more frustrated I became with the humility of my lifestyle as a monk. I guess it showed, because one day I was walking down to the monks' kitchen, and as I passed by one of the senior monks (who'd been in the monastery 45 years), he muttered, "A bird should not say, 'I will be a dog.'"

He knew I was in denial about my life there. It's a great life, but a person has to really love structure. I had 120 brothers, yet I felt completely isolated. And the day came when I just couldn't deal with my life like that anymore.

A few weeks later that same old monk called a meeting for me with the senior monks:

"Greg, you're struggling here. This is not the right place for you. You're so ambitious."

"Well, there's room here to be ambitious," I replied.

"Yeah, but you have your own will and you have things you want to do and you can't do them and it's frustrating. This is a life of surrender and it's really not cut out for you," he said.

"I came here to give my life to God and although I'm going through a little bit of psychological stress right now, and I don't care if I end up drooling in a wheelchair, I've given my life to God and it's not mine, it's His. So whatever God wants me to do, I'll do."

And the senior monk sat back in his chair and said, "Oh, I understand now. You have two weeks." I was in shock. "You'll be leaving on April 2," he continued. My first reaction was, "What did I do wrong?" And he answered, "I want to make this real clear to you. You have never broken a single vow or a single rule as a monk. You're an exemplary monk. It's not about that. It's about temperament—you having work to do and it's not here."

And so I found myself 35 years old, sitting in front of the gates of the monastery and waiting to embark on another one of life's journey. I reminisced how eight years earlier, I had driven through those gates in the opposite direction. Eight years earlier, as I entered through those gates, I heard this beautiful voice—I've heard God's voice just twice in my life—coming from everywhere and it was the most reassuring experience of my life. The voice said, "Welcome home." And yet here I was now, sitting in a rental car packed with everything I owned, parked inside those gates facing out, asking myself, "Where am I going to go? This is home!?"

I sat there for 30 minutes thinking, "I can't just sit here. I'll just pull through those gates and pull over and sob, I guess." I started the car and rolled toward the gates and all of a sudden, a wave of joy just rolled through me and I was practically giggling. This was the exact opposite of anything I had expected and a sense of peace came over me and I heard the same voice saying the same words, "Welcome home." I went, in a matter of seconds, from feeling totally broken down and not knowing what to do or where to go to feeling a sense of freedom and joy.

I found myself driving down the road singing and ready to join that huge world ... for which I had only contempt. Wait! What was I thinking? The world's not a nice place. I had joined the monastery years before to escape the world. In fact, a lot of people join a monastery or convent because they're trying to find a back door to sneak out of life.

But by the time I got to the bottom of the hill five minutes later, I had it figured out—I was going to China, India and Japan. I'd never visited India, and I'd heard it was a very spiritual place. But I'd known China and Japan were godless, materialistic and communistic environments, and now I had to face all those judgments I had created.

So I visited those places and met extraordinary, beautiful people—moral, spiritual people—and proved to myself that there's no place where God is not present.

When I returned home, I experienced my second midlife crisis—now what do I do? I had ambition but no preparation for being out in the world. But I knew one thing— I loved to listen. In the monastery that's what we did. Twelve thousand hours were devoted to silent meditation. Eventually, all your senses shut down and you become very self-aware of the very deep levels of concentration. I had mastered a very specific skill: listening. With that experience in mind, I decided I wanted to teach people how to listen.

By now I had married, and I discussed it with my wife and asked her for ideas. At the time, she was teaching classes at The Learning Annex on interior design and how to open a health spa, and she suggested that I start there.

For a year and a half I offered a class, along with a workbook and a tape, called "Spiritual Communication," and it was designed for primary relationships—mother-daughter, husband-wife, brother-sister, etc. Then I joined Toastmasters, an organization devoted to developing public speaking and leadership skills through practice and feedback. I was asked to speak there as well as at UCLA and USC.

Unfortunately, I discovered that most people just can't listen, even with the tools I was giving them. And it was frustrating for me. Then one day my wife asked, "You've changed people's lives. Why are you unsatisfied?" "It's so frustrating when I see how much deeper people could go" I told her. And she said, "Figure out why they can't get past it."

So I did. But before I tell you, why do you think people don't listen? Because they have something they want to say and they're just waiting for the other person to shut up before they can say it? Because they're daydreaming? Nope. It's because they lack self-confidence—the reason people don't listen is because they don't know where they stand and so they feel threatened by those that do. So I started to pay attention to my clients' internal conversations: What was meaningful to them? Where did they stand? And I used the tools I learned in listening so that when somebody spoke, I would process it through body language, voice tone and all that—and process not just what they said, but where they were speaking from.

And soon I realized what I was doing had a lot to do with my discoveries in the monastery where I studied eastern philosophy, folklore, Christianity, mythology and the *Mahabharata* (an ancient Sanskrit epic). All these paths of wisdom had heroes; take the Mahabharata for example—there are all these warrior kings, like Yudhisthira, who is the incarnation of truth and walks with his feet one inch off the ground everywhere he goes because he's so elevated by his commitment to truth. And one day he tells a small lie to win a battle, and his feet slowly touch down to the ground and he has to walk with his feet on the ground forever.

And I looked at the hero's journey, where somebody comes up against something greater than himself (like a dragon), and he has to find something within himself and call it forward, discovering powers that allow him to conquer or even saddle the dragon. And he's the hero because he's full of virtue—self-trust, confidence and loyalty. And so, through listening I discovered that behind every person's behaviors, beliefs and values, there are virtues. I call them Heart Virtues, because they tend to live in a person's heart (not their head).

I noticed that corporations, even, have mission statements and say things like "we promote honesty, integrity," or, "to become the leader through teamwork" etc.—those are virtues. And I started understanding that this is really the fabric of humanity.

So I developed a program and called it "Heart Virtues." When a person learns what his or her heart virtue is, all of a sudden everything starts making sense. "Why do my relationships work?" "Why don't my relationships work?" "Why am I a particular way about people and things in my life?" I have found that when people discover who they are, what they really represent to the world, and what is most important to them, they can use this knowledge and their inherent talents to increase their productivity and wealth, and most important of all—create, at will, more fulfilling experiences in life ... if they live authentically from the inside out, instead of living from the outside in, burying what's most meaningful to them and how much they truly care about others.

I discovered that listening creates a seductive vacuum, which invites people to blossom and awaken to their ambitions. And that when they learn who they are and where they stand, they can listen to anybody say anything—and open the space for others to blossom. The first step is to know who we truly are, and that is the immediate gift of Learning Our Heart Virtue. That's the title of my first book, *Learn Our Heart Virtue, To Be Who We Are.*

Now in addition to a flourishing private practice, I train coaches, give lectures and empower those who suffer from my past pains: not knowing their true career and how to have beautiful, powerful relationships.

You and I came here for a reason—to make a contribution, for which we will be highly rewarded. I am convinced that you are already on your true path ... you already care when things fall apart and strive to improve everything and everyone around you. Simply own those ambitions, and take one small act of courage toward them every day.

Chapter 3

A DAUGHTER'S PROMISE

"Stay in the moment."

– Unknown

By Pamela Doyal Bruce & Nancy Irwin

I N 1973, I COMPLETED my bachelor's degree in interior design from Auburn University's School of Architecture. I subsequently worked for corporate design firms, managed the design department of a major corporate furniture dealer, and established a consulting firm to work with corporations in all aspects of corporate design.

Thirty years is a long time to be in one profession—especially for someone like me with an entrepreneurial spirit and the desire for new challenges—so I knew the day would arrive when I would want to move beyond corporate design and put my skills and talents to another use.

In 1999, while working in the interior management department at Turner Properties in Atlanta, I applied and was accepted into the Georgia State University Gerontology Centers graduate program. My interest focused on "aging in place." Each course assisted me in understanding the psychology, physiology and sociology of aging. My goal was to apply my knowledge of design to enhance safety, comfort and independence for the elderly in new or existing homes.

With our country's rapidly aging population, I knew I could always find work in the gerontology profession; however, I wasn't exactly sure how I would apply my knowledge and when I would make the transition. Eventually, I stopped trying so hard. The answer came to me thanks to my dad. Before he passed away in 2005, I promised my father that I would keep his company, Villa Rica Knitters, running and keep his employees. His main concern was keeping the senior workers. Because of gerontology studies, I knew that most of them would, most likely, not be able to find another job.

And I knew that, with my father gone, the mill needed me. My 81-year-old mother, a breast cancer survivor who's legally blind, needed me too.

I didn't have time to go through a long decision-making process. I had a purpose to fulfill at the mill and with my mother. After quickly weighing the pros and cons, I stepped up to the plate. Everything was in place at the mill except a president. I determined that the most capable and obvious person to take on the job would be me.

In hindsight, all the jobs I held in my previous design career prepared me for this—creating and designing new products, managing employees and projects, learning sales and marketing, and developing an understanding of what it takes to run and manage a business.

Of course, I had to stay positive when I thought about becoming the president of Villa Rica Knitters. My initial concerns centered on whether the company would succeed or fail once I took over. And, of course, I had feelings about returning to my hometown, Villa Rica,

Georgia. After graduating from high school in 1969, I couldn't wait to go away to college and move to the big city. Could I really go back? Yes, I could. I had a solid base of friends who supported me in the decision, I had succeeded in the corporate design profession and I was confident of who I had become.

After I settled in and had a chance to study all aspects of the business, I observed many obstacles that felt overwhelming: the rising price of acrylic yarn (which is made from petroleum), difficulty in finding new employees due to a work force that's becoming obsolete, offshore manufacturing competition with whose prices we cannot begin to compete, and balancing finances as we manufacture seasonal products.

The thought of 13 employees being laid off and most likely not being hired is the predominant force that keeps me going. Eight of the employees are 63 to 81, have very few marketable skills and would have a difficult time finding another job. One year everyone received a holiday bonus, and some employees received salary increases—which was as rewarding for me as it was for them

If I had to do it all over again, I would. I enjoy my work at the mill and realize that I am putting my marketing, management and design skills to use. Even more important, I couldn't let my dad or his company down. My dad, as well as the people who worked with him for 22 years to create Villa Rica Knitters, are my role models. They worked very hard and applied their knowledge of the knitting industry to create this business. The employees who arrive at work at 7 every morning with a positive attitude and proud to be employed here are also role models; they give me the drive to continue working.

But my main fear was and is failure. What will happen to the employees if the mill closes due to my leadership? That thought truly pushes me onward to the next marketing call and the next one after that. The thought is with me when I drive almost two hours most days to the factory, when I hear sales rejections due mainly to price and offshore competition, and when I get discouraged when the rent and operating expenses go up.

Our philosophy is to "do the best we can every day and stay in the moment rather than worry about the future," and it seems to be working. We continue to think of new ways to market and define our niche. All of the employees are dedicated and the hard work is paying off. We are keeping existing accounts and finding new accounts as well as increasing profits, staying out of debt and keeping the work force working!

If fear raises its ugly head, I have several words of advice I'd like to share with you: listen to your inner voice and address the doubts it's saying, have a strong support group that will listen (but do not abuse this privilege), study the market and be sure your new profession has a future, set aside time for yourself and personal life, and do not let work absorb you. Finally, if this transition does not work, let it go and move on to the next one.

You may want to ask yourself a few questions before making a midlife transition:

1. What are the worst and best things that can happen?
2. Am I financially prepared to make this transition?
3. Do I have medical, disability and other insurance assurances in place?
4. Is the timing in my life right?
5. Am I rushing into this transition?
6. Should I be better prepared before making this transition?

Timing is everything when making a transition, and the timing was right for me to take on this challenge. Every day I'm reminded of the promise I made to my dad and feel fortunate to be blessed with the spirit and courage to keep his legacy alive. My dad would be so proud of what we've accomplished.

Chapter 4

SOMETIMES YOU HAVE TO ASK GOD FOR A SIGN

"If only God would give me a clear sign!
Like making a large deposit in my name at a Swiss bank!"
– Woody Allen

By Chellie Campbell

FOR MONTHS, MY AGENT, Lisa Hagan, and I searched for a publisher for my first book, *The Wealthy Spirit*. Many rejections and several almost-deals later, I still didn't have a publisher. At one time, I had a deal with HarperSanFrancisco—they published a series of page-a-day books like *365 Dao* and *365 Goddess*, and thought my page-a-day format about money would really fit in with that. I was so excited! I celebrated, called all my friends and announced it at my LeTip business networking breakfast. Everyone cheered for my success. Four days later, the publisher cancelled the deal because its parent company, Harper Collins in New York, had just signed another person's page-a-day money book. So not only had I lost the deal, but someone else had developed my same idea and was going to be the first one to market with it. I was destroyed over it ... for a day or two.

And then I decided that no way could this other woman write MY book because MY book was MY story of MY life, and no one else could do that. I got back to work and back to practicing my positive publishing affirmations (example: "My book is a *New York Times* bestseller, helps many people, inspires and entertains readers, and easily makes me rich and famous!"). I knew that my book was good and that I could write, so I knew in my bones I would find a publisher. Okay, not this one. Jack Canfield, co-author of the "Chicken Soup" series, told me the four-letter word to use when someone rejects you: "Next!" I would not give up.

There are times you have to decide when to hold 'em and when to fold 'em. You fold 'em when you feel finished, when you no longer have passion for the work, when you don't see that other people are benefiting from your work. You fold 'em when the price tag is too high and the rewards not good enough. But you hold on when you love what you do, when you believe in yourself, when others believe in you and benefit from your work. Delay is not defeat—when the world crushes you and it all gets too hard, you get in bed, turn the electric blanket up and eat chocolate. But only for a day. Then you remember that people are praying for you to show up and help them, and you get up and help them. And by helping them, you help yourself.

Meanwhile, a friend from my writers group had the most glorious success. Rhonda Britten prepared her proposal and met with nine publishers; her book went up for auction, and she got a six-figure advance! I was truly happy for her and celebrated her success. But I couldn't help asking God, "Hey, what about me?"

I was willing to do whatever it took to get a publisher. Lisa told me most of the publishers disliked the original page-a-day structure. So I revised the proposal and rewrote the book as an eight-chapter narrative. I changed the packaging and paid to have a matching cover design for my audio and videotapes. The new packages went out to publishers, and once again, Lisa and I waited.

In the meantime, I had a conversation with God and asked him for a sign. I told him I had done everything I knew how to do, and now I needed him to clearly show me if this goal, this book, was meant for me. I let him know that I am here to do his work, and that I was willing to get my poor human ego out of the way and give this up, if that was what he wanted me to do. But I needed a clear sign whether or not to keep trying. God has three answers to prayers: "Yes," "Not now" and "I have something better for you."

Exactly two days later, Deb Werksman at Sourcebooks called to say she was interested in my book. We discussed the narrative version, and then she asked, "What's this page-a-day book that your agent told me about? She says everyone in her office uses it." After I described it to her, she said, "I want to see *that* book." It wasn't long before I got another call from her: "I just got out of an acquisitions meeting and we would love to publish your book!"

And you know what? They bought the original version!

God's on duty 24/7. He's just waiting for you to *ask*.

And now here I am five years later (after filing bankruptcy at age 46 and starting completely over in life), with two published books and countless magazine articles to my credit; I'm a lecturer and I've been quoted in 15 books. And, of course, I was thrilled when I was asked to contribute to *You-Turn*.

I even have a blog on Amazon.com that typifies my belief that we can harness the energies of the universe and embrace the hidden potential that lives inside us all. I've added one of my blogs here because I strongly believe in the power of attraction and positive thinking, and it may help you ignite your burning desires.

6 Degrees of Jack Canfield

Do you know how The Law of Attraction works? You hold the vision of what you want and invest it with feelings of joy and success as though it was already yours.

I held the vision of having a story in one of Jack Canfield's books. I knew Jack from years before, when we were in a networking group in the late '80s. Later, when I started writing my first book, *The Wealthy Spirit*, I went to the "How to Build Your Speaking and Writing Empire" seminar he put on with Mark Victor Hansen, and reintroduced myself. Our paths would cross from time to time after that—I'd see him at BookExpo America, I'd go to his book signings, I'd see him speak at an event, we even ran into each other on an airplane. I didn't have a plan for us to work together; I just saw held the vision.

One day a year or so ago, I got an email from Jack's office, asking me if I would like to submit a story for *You've Got to Read This Book!* I was delighted and wrote about a wonderful book that transformed my life, *When I Say No, I Feel Guilty* by Manuel Smith. I was ecstatic when the editor, Carol Kline, called to tell me they liked my story and it was included in the book.

I asked then, how had I been selected to receive an invitation to contribute a story, telling her of the many times I had crossed paths with Jack. But that wasn't it. What had happened was that a woman in Jack's office was reading *How to Run Your Business Like a Girl* by Elizabeth Cogswell Baskin, and called to invite Elizabeth to write a story. Elizabeth had profiled me in her book because she had been reading *The Wealthy Spirit*. She said to Jack's associate, "Have you invited Chellie? You've got to ask Chellie!" And so I got my invitation.

The Law of Attraction always works. You will always receive your vision. It may not come in the way you expect—all the logical steps may not work out at all. But it will come. Trust and believe.

Chapter 5

YOU GOTTA STAY STRONG

"Keep pushin' on. Things are going to get better."

– Boom

By Vickie Strogin & Nancy Irwin

BEFORE I FOUND MY success, I had hit rock bottom. I was a high school dropout, drug addict and ex-convict. Despair, hopelessness and tragedy were a part of my everyday life. But as they say, "Success is how high you bounce after you hit rock bottom."

Every time I took two steps forward, someone would come along and try to knock me one step back. People used me, lied to me, cheated me, conned me, deserted me and stole from me. But I never felt sorry for myself. I just kept on pushin' ahead. No matter how bad things got, I always believed that I could fight my way out of anything. I'm a fighter, always have been.

I'm the youngest of four kids; each one of us had a different father. We were raised in the projects of South Central in Los Angeles by an alcoholic mother, who did the best she could. My mother loved her children and did everything in her power to raise us right. With no stability in our lives, we all chose our own paths. My two older brothers turned to gangs, and my sister turned to the streets. Just as I was starting high school, my mother abandoned us, saying the stress was too much for her to handle.

With no responsible adult in the house, I took it upon myself to raise my sister's little boy. We were all evicted three or four months after my mother left. Eventually, she got herself together and came back, and life went on as before.

A car was the most important thing to me when I turned 16, and I asked my mother for money so I could buy one. Of course, she didn't have the money, but I was so determined, I worked two jobs one summer and bought my first car myself. As I look back on it, I can't believe that I wasn't aware of my own determination.

At 18, I went to work for my dad in the restaurant he owned. I didn't really know him. I'd see him every once in a while, but the only time I'd talk to him was when my mother put me on the phone to ask him for money. She would tell me what to say. Her philosophy was, "If we need $100, ask for $200," because he would always cut it down anyway.

After working with my dad for a while, I really got to know him and moved in with him. Six months later, someone came in to the restaurant, stabbed him and killed him.

My dad had three kids with other women, and when he died they all got together with my mother and asked, "Who's going to run this restaurant?" Everybody pitched in, but one by one they all fell out until it was just me. I was the only person who knew anything about the business. Eventually, I took on all the responsibilities and transferred everything into my name.

Imagine, I'm 19 years old, never graduated high school, and here I am owning and running a business! Knowing how important it was to be a financial success, I made a room in the back and lived and slept there to save money. If my car broke down, I'd catch the bus and travel back and forth from downtown to the restaurant, picking up and delivering supplies and anything else I needed.

The restaurant opened every day at 10 a.m. and closed at 2 in the morning. To learn more about the business, I attended classes at a technical college, studying restaurant management every morning before I opened it up for customers. So there I was, frying chicken all day, all night—and going to school in the morning.

I struggled like this for a few years, and the day finally came when I felt totally trapped. I'd look out the restaurant window and see people my age coming and going and doing as they pleased. Maybe they were going to the beach or a movie, or just taking it easy. I felt tired, frustrated and lonely. Then my cousin began working with me—and introduced me to crack. The first time I did it, I felt the room spin out of control, but I continued to do it because it was an escape. It was a chance to get away from the responsibility of the restaurant, the grief from my father's death and all the pressures I had placed on myself to succeed. I kept doing crack a little at a time until I was hooked.

It went on like this for years, and there I was, still fighting to make the restaurant a success and still living in that room in the back. At 25, it hit me—I had spent the last seven years of my life in that restaurant. I was looking for a way out when one day, a couple of businessmen asked me about sub-leasing the property. I quickly agreed.

My father had owned a couple of houses, and after he died, my sister and I got $25,000 when they sold. So with that money, plus the income from sub-leasing the restaurant, I went out and got my first apartment. By the time I was 27, I was hooked on crack and knew I had to get help. I'd blown almost all the money but had just enough to get into a drug rehab program. I stayed there for three months, but it didn't work for me; once I was back home, I started doing crack again.

With no money with no place to live, I turned to a friend who owned a junkyard. Together we'd collect bottles, cans and aluminum, take it all to a recycler, then go buy crack with the money. Our routine was 8 to 4 every day. I lived in a van in his junkyard for a year.

All the time I was living like this, I knew I had to be responsible and take care of myself. I tried to clean up and get a job, but the drug kept calling me. Yet I never stole to support my habit—I can at least be proud of that. The next step for most was prostitution, but me, I started dealing.

The whole time, believe it or not, I kept my optimism. I was always saying, "Come on, we got to make it, we got to win, we got to try something." I continued to go to church because I knew that there was something God wanted me to do with my life. Many times, I'd sit in church and cry. I always felt bad about what I was doing; I knew it was wrong.

Then one day, I got arrested for selling cocaine and went to jail. I was 28 years old, and it was the best thing to ever happen to me. The judge sentenced me to six months and told me that if I ever appeared in front of him again, he'd give me five years in prison.

After I got out on probation I went back to my old neighborhood, terrified that if I started using or selling crack again, I'd be going to prison for five years. It was at that time I made one of the hardest decisions of my life. I called my probation officer and told her that I wanted to get clean and get help. She gave me phone numbers to various drug rehab programs, and I made arrangements to join one.

During the years I was on crack, I lived in dirty, run-down, empty houses, apartment buildings, bus benches and cars, and here was my chance—maybe my last chance—to start over. When I entered the building and the doors closed behind me, I remember thinking to myself, "I don't want to go back out there."

While in drug rehab I did everything I was told. If they told me to scrub the floor with a toothbrush, I would. However, I knew I needed a job. I didn't have a skill, but I had discipline. All the discipline I had running the restaurant plus all the hustling I put into selling drugs was now going to pay off and push me to be something bigger and better. By now I was 33 and learning that I could be my best friend or worst enemy.

Finally drug free, I got a telemarketing job paying $5 an hour. Every day I'd tell myself, "You're not going to lose this job." By sheer will and hard work, I was the No. 1 producer in my first month. Slowly I went from $5 to $7 an hour. When the company relocated, I was asked to move with them. By now I was making $8 an hour and getting bonuses because I continued to be a top producer. Five years later, at age 38, I was promoted to assistant manager, making $400 a week working two shifts and Saturdays.

One day the company's sales representative and I started talking about real estate. We didn't know anything about it, but we started calling companies and telling them we were real estate investors. All I knew was that real estate was—and is—profitable.

At this time, my boss told me that he was going to open another office and was looking for people to train the new employees. I told him that if he helped me buy a house, I would train the people for free. He agreed and I set about working as a trainer, telemarketer and assistant.

Sounds like a lot of work, but I was only making $8 an hour! After all the taxes and everything were taken out, I'd bring home $500 every other week, so I really watched my money. My rent was $500 a month, so that didn't leave me much money for anything else. I used candles to keep electric bill cheap. I didn't have cable. If I needed anything, I bought it at a pawn shop. For groceries, I'd buy food at the dollar store or eat once or twice a day at a fast-food restaurant off the dollar menu.

Soon word got out that I was really good at telemarketing, and I was recommended for a job at another company. Now I had five people working for me, but I was still telemarketing myself. The pay was the same but the hours were better. I worked there from 8 a.m. to 3 p.m., and then from 5 to 9 p.m., I'd go to Bryman College, where I worked setting up appointments for people who were interested in taking courses.

In 1996, I decided to buy my first house. This was right after the 1994 Northridge earthquake, and the housing prices were lower. I started calling a few people, including my old boss who originally said he'd help me, and I got enough money for a down payment. He signed all the paperwork, and then I owned a house!

But I was still working the same hours at the telemarketing company and college, and making house repairs in-between. By 1999, I realized that the house was taking up all my time and money, so I decided to rent it out.

I used that money to buy two condos, and then real estate offers started rolling in. No, not offers to buy my properties; everyone was offering me a job—the escrow company, the title company, the agent who sold me my first house— everybody! They all thought I was really motivated and aggressive. It was then that I decided maybe real estate was my calling, so I studied to get my real estate license.

At this point I was making $700 a week but still saving my money and eating from the dollar store. Then opportunity knocked. My best friend's aunt had two properties in foreclosure. Because I had good credit, I got a loan, bought them and rented them out.

I began working part-time at a real estate funding company selling houses but wouldn't give up the stability of my telemarketing job. By now, I was making $2000 a month and starting to feel that I was wasting my time sitting on the phone. Was I going to work as a telemarketer until I was 60? I kept asking myself, "What else can I do to make $2000 a month?"

Because my life was turning around, I wanted to give something back. I promised myself that the next house I bought would have a purpose. I kept that promise with a two-story Victorian that boasted six bedrooms, a family room and a big back yard. I turned the house into a Sober Living residence, a group home for men who need help getting off their addictions.

Once I bought the house I asked, "How am I going to get people in here?" First, I placed ads in the paper. Then, I used my skills as a telemarketer to call all the drug programs, telling them I had a Sober

Living house. I also went to the parole offices and put up flyers. Word got out slowly, and the calls started coming in. I got tenants over the next six to eight months. Then, like now, people paid a fair rent for room and board in my shelters, and in return they had a clean and safe place to stay. With my street knowledge, I understood the people who lived in my homes and understood their problems.

I turned one of my condos into a Sober Living shelter when the man who rented it skipped town after being wanted by the police.

I never really make any money with the Sober Living business—the real estate supports those places. I sell a place and I take that money, buy another one and fix the place up. I love doing it. I love helping people. I love giving people my energy, my motivation and all that.

And through it all, I never forgot my family; I took care of my mother, my brothers, and my nephew and his children. But once again, tragedy came into my life when my nephew died from a gunshot wound.

I'm now 45 years old. In addition to buying and maintaining my group homes, I own a motel and an apartment building. I also give motivational speeches at the parole board for recent parolees, and I love doing that. I truly believe in helping people and that I'm helping God fulfill the promise to the world that we are all here to watch out for one another.

I never really had a support system; I've always listened to motivational speakers because they have done the things I want to do. I take their strength and the things they've done to motivate me to do better. When I was a telemarketer, my cubicle was filled with motivational sayings. I would read this stuff over and over to give me strength. I was and am filled with ambition, hope and dreams.

To succeed, you have to work hard, turn off the TV, get off the couch and go do it. After all these years, I found my own personal keys to success:

1. **Financial Discipline**: The restaurant taught me how to sacrifice. When I got clean, I still had that discipline with money. I saved and saved and didn't spend it away on things I didn't need. I sacrificed and put the money back into the business.

2. **Action:** You have to have energy. My energy at midnight is the same during the day; I'm always up and ready to go. I wasted so many years on drugs; I told myself, "One-third of your life is over, and it's never coming back, and so you better get busy." I feel like I made up for these years by getting my life in motion. When the judge told me I could land in jail for five years, that really turned me around. I knew I had to take action and do something with my life.

3. **Have a Good Heart:** You have to help people. I made a conscious choice not to lie or cheat. And no matter what people have done to me, I am grateful for everything good that has happened to me.

4. **Believe in Yourself and Your Dreams:** I didn't know if any of this would work. But I had to believe. People laughed at me as I was trying to make my life better, and pushing myself toward something bigger and brighter. Well, they're not laughing now. In fact, now they want to be my friend.

If I had to do it all over again, I would. Each step took me to the next opportunity and the next one and the next one and brought me to where I am today. My advice to others who grew up in similar circumstances is to realize that we are not here to just live and die. If you've been through something, listen to that annoying little voice that's deep inside you—that's God, your conscience, telling you to do what's right. And you have to believe that it's going to take a lot of time. You can't just go from 0 to 100 in a second.

I will always remember the sacrifices and the promises I made to myself to never give up, to just hang on for one more day. To keep me going, motivated and inspired, in my darkest times and my most happy, I'd sing my favorite song to remind me where I'm going and why:

I kick around, there's no money to be found
Sometimes I think I'll never find no peace of mind
Sometimes I think I'm gonna leave you all behind
Keep pushin' on
Things are going to get better
Keep movin' on

Keep on reaching to the top
Keep on movin' movin'
Keep pushin' on
You'll go higher, baby, higher, baby
Keep movin' on
Keep pushin' on
Things are going to get better
It won't take long
Keep on pushin' to the top
I tell ya brother, where there's a will there's a way
Keep pushin' on,
Keep movin' on
If you reach a little deeper you'll go higher, higher.

— Keep Pushin' by Boom

Chapter 6

SOMETIMES THE BEST VISIONS
EMERGE FROM HARD TIMES

*"Dare to dream, to speak the language of your heart, to shape its
longings into clear visions with solid goals and objectives."*

– Pat McHenry Sullivan

By Pat McHenry Sullivan

A S A SPIRIT AND work consultant, author and speaker, I help
people bring more integrity, purpose and joy into any task.
This work is wonderfully varied, reaching all faiths and all
types of jobs. Recently I've written an article for a legal journal; helped
create business plans for several creative businesses; set the winter 2008
schedule for the Spirit and Work Resource Center my husband John

and I founded; and advised several women how to design their own vision quest.

When I made my you-turn at age 45—trading life as a freelance writer in Washington, D.C., for a graduate program in spirituality and psychology in Oakland, California—only the visioning part of my work was foreseen. The rest happened after I failed, then made the best of some very hard times.

In grad school in 1987, I wove together training from Barbara Sher, author of *I Could Do Anything I Want If I Only Knew What It was*, with many gifts from my parents on how to shape a dream into a practical plan. I grounded this in their teachings: "Get out in the world and let it teach you. Honor creativity as a gift from God and a call from God. Be true to yourself, even if integrity is an unpopular course."

Into this, I had planted the fruits of decades of study in spirituality and psychology, particularly a body-based therapy called bioenergetics, and all I had learned from dealing with the grief of my mother's death when I was only 13. Until I built a visioning business, I planned to use strategies that previously had generated writing clients. Meanwhile, my husband would work as a police dispatcher as he continued to seek his new vocational visions.

When none of these plans worked, I fell back on paralegal or legal secretarial work. Around 1991, I took a full-time job as a floater (an in-house "temp") for a large law firm and dreamed that one day clients for my "true work" would appear.

Shortly after that, John's dad had a stroke. He lived, unable to eat or speak, for three years. Around the same time, we learned John's brother-in-law was dying of liver cancer and that my beloved stepmother, Violet, had colon cancer. With all our family on the East Coast, it took a lot of overtime on my part to keep us in airline tickets. For several years, all my vacation time was arranged around Violet's surgeries.

The dream that had brought us to California kept moving further away. Then four breakthroughs happened that eventually realized the dream in surprising ways.

Breakthrough No. 1 started after I picked up the local newspaper of various consciousness programs and practitioners. Inside the front cover was a full-page, full-color ad for Barbara Brennan, a long-ago colleague in bioenergetics who had realized her dream big-time. Her New York healing school was offering a new program in San Francisco. Her second book was coming out.

My jealousy quickly turned into self-deprecation. She was a success; I was nothing but a legal secretary with a huge student loan, few prospects and the inability to buy a tiny ad.

When I turned to Oprah for solace, I got even more jealous when I saw that one of her guests was another friend, Olivia Mellan, talking about her second book!

Fortunately, the Pathwork training all of us had shared took over. As I poured out feelings and tensions, I accepted the fact that my own lack of faith, not outside forces, was quashing my dreams. I remembered a lecture from the Pathwork (www.Pathwork.org). Pay attention to your jealousy, it said. Find under your judgments and comparisons your essential call. For me that meant, like Barbara and Livvy, to build a career on what mattered most to me and to affect people for the better. That day I vowed to do whatever was necessary to be true to the call that had brought me to graduate school, however that call reshaped itself. For the first night in months, I slept well.

Breakthrough No. 2 came when I realized that to stay efficient enough to keep my job in the new era of downsizings, I had to bring my spiritual practices to my work. That meant blessing my work, being grateful for it and discovering allies who always had time for a quick hug and didn't expect a "fine!" when they asked, "how are you?" As I learned how to work more efficiently, I sometimes came home with more energy at the end of the day than I'd had in the beginning. I was better able to deal with all that was happening in John's and my family.

Breakthrough No. 3 came in December 1995, the day of the firm's annual Christmas party. Just as I was putting on my coat to go home and prepare for the festivities, the senior partner whose office was in sight of my desk yelled, "Come here, Pat!"

"How rude," I thought. When I entered her office, she was on the phone with a client. She pointed to her left. I looked, but found no work to do. I finally understood she wanted me to look out the window. That made me mad. I'm running late and she wants me to look out the window?

Finally, I saw the magnificent rainbow hanging over San Francisco Bay. "Thank you," I mouthed, looking back at the partner. She smiled and went on advising her client.

As I took in the beauty of the rainbow, time and pressure lost their grip on my belly. I felt ashamed of how easily I had broken the first rule of law, "never assume," and how quickly false assumptions had made me think ill of another. Then I felt a strong sense of blessing and grace. The only way I knew to deal with my awe was to return to my desk and pray.

All around, people bustled. As I prayed, I remembered the solstice ceremony invitations in my purse. For years, my husband and I had held this ancient ceremony to honor the wisdom of darkness, of pain, of not having immediate answers.

In my prayer, I got a clear message, "invite Mr. X to the solstice." How could this be, I wondered. Mr. X was one of the most conservative attorneys on staff and highly unlikely to appreciate a solstice invitation. He also had been crabby and difficult to work for recently.

But the prayer message was as clear as the rainbow had been beautiful. Nervously, I got up and knocked on Mr. X's door. He answered gruffly. I went in, smiled and offered the invitation, then said a few things about what it meant.

"I need this, though I can't come," he finally said. "My wife's mother is dying, and my wife is trying to take care of everything, including our little children. They don't understand it all; they just want it to be happy like Christmas is supposed to be."

Again, I grew ashamed at how quickly assumptions had blocked my ability to see larger truths. After some brief but mutual well-wishing, the attorney went back to work, and I passed out the rest of the invitations and went home to prepare for the party.

Later, I thanked the partner who had shown me the rainbow. "No big deal," she said. "I just noticed it and knew you would appreciate it." But it was a big deal, for the moment at the window broke past the grief in my heart and created room where new vision could grow.

Within months, John had a new job as research director for the first-ever major spirit and work resource guide. Though I'd never heard the term "spirit and work," its concepts were totally aligned with all my parents had taught me.

Through contacts John gave me, I got the assignment to photograph "workplace altars," showing many ways people keep spirit alive at work, for a meeting of the Bay Area Organizational Network. Some of my favorite pictures came from that law firm. Within a year, I would talk openly about the heart and soul of the legal profession and seek a way to help heal that heart and soul.

Law is often considered picky and unfeeling, but it's based on the same truths that anchor all spiritual disciplines. Working for lawyers taught me to serve someone I dislike at least as well as someone I like very much. It's taught me that meaningful work doesn't depend on job description but on giving each task my best, and on using all work to learn about myself and to serve others. And as that moment with Mr. X taught me, I don't have to fear speaking a prayerful thought, no matter how strange it first appears.

After that, the breakthroughs kept coming. I dared to submit an article to the *San Francisco Chronicle's* career section, then to pitch and sell a regular column on spirit and work. Internet research for "spirituality and law" led me to Stewart Levine, a prominent mediator and author of *Getting to Resolution* and other books. When he invited me to be part of a Future Search visioning process in Chicago for the American Bar Association, I networked with my columns. Over breakfast one morning during the Future Search, I was invited by a publisher's scout to write the book, *Work with Meaning, Work with Joy: Bringing Your Spirit to Any Job.*

At 65, I am just hitting my stride in my work. John and I, who now work well together, are looking forward to our 25th wedding anniversary in the spring. The best advice I can give anyone who wants to find and live their own visions is to heed a call that came to me in a meditation during one of those terribly hard times:

Dare to dream, to speak the language of your heart,
to shape its longings into clear visions with
solid goals and objectives.
Dare to do, to craft your visions with integrity,
and the joy of stretching your skills far beyond
their original capacity.

Chapter 7

ALL THE POSSIBILITIES

"Hope is a good thing, maybe the best of things.
And no good thing ever dies."

– The Shawshank Redemption

By Carl Weisman

A FTER ALMOST 20 YEARS in the field of engineering and sales engineering, I finally landed what I thought was a great job; it was a job I could be proud of and one that paid very well. I was hired as the director of sales and marketing at a small technology company in Marina Del Rey, California, a small coastal village located on Los Angeles's Westside. All was going well and I sincerely thought that *this* would be the last stop in my career—a place where I could grow old and retire. There was only one problem: about a year after I was hired, I was fired. Let's just say that there was a clash of wills with the owner ... and we know who always wins that one.

So there I was, with a $400,000 mortgage and no money in the bank and no income. I scrambled to assemble a resume and quickly put together a couple of job interviews. What a shock when I went to my second interview—I was sitting across from someone whom 1 should have been interviewing to work for *me*. Plus, the job offered a compensation package that would have barely allowed me to make ends meet with my new mortgage. Then it hit me—I realized that if I took the job, I would literally be working just to keep the house! So I made a decision that would forever and dramatically change the course of my life.

I decided that, rather than work for someone who should have been working for me at a salary that was less than what I needed (and was worth), I said "*#?! it" and I took the other road.

First thing to go was the house. It sold at a profit that allowed me to live for a while with no financial concerns. Next, I moved back to my old neighborhood and into a small two-bedroom apartment. I still had no job, no income and no prospects, but I had something I had never had before: a sense of possibility. While I was searching for work, I started a consulting business; it helped out, but only in the short term. In the meantime, I wrote a best-selling book on technology, *The Essential Guide to RF & Wireless* (Prentice Hall) that allowed me to conduct public seminars, which was another way to make ends meet.

Over the next five years, I drifted from one short-term gig to another. Along the way I managed to work in the healthcare field, the real estate industry, the dot-com world (of course), the wireless industry and the direct marketing area, and I managed to write the second edition of my book. Of course, none of these jobs paid enough, so I supplemented what I made with my savings; but after five years it was gone. There I was again, with no steady job and no savings—the sense of possibility was becoming a burden. But what I lacked in assets I made up for in experience.

With money and time running out, I was forced to consider going back to do the only thing for which I was really qualified: engineering. After a few months' search, I was fortunate to land a job close to home. It paid well enough to cover the bills, but it did something else: it gave me a chance to write. I wrote white papers and articles, many of which were ultimately published in trade journals. And somewhere along the way, writing at that job, it hit me: I love to write! That's why I'm here. At age 49, I have discovered that I was meant to be a writer. And that is exactly what I'm doing now: promoting my latest book, *So, Why Have You Never Been Married? Conversations with Never Married Men Over 40*, and working on the next.

I don't know how successful it will become, but I enjoy the process of writing so much, it doesn't really matter. The payoff is in the journey.

Chapter 8

HITTING ALL THE RIGHT NOTES

"Music is enough for a lifetime, but a lifetime is not enough for music."
– Rachmaninoff

By Louise Barfield & Nancy Irwin

M USIC HAS BEEN THE inspiration of my life since I was a child. My mother, grandmother and great-grandmother had each earned degrees or certificates in music, so it was only natural that rhythm, melody and harmony would play a starring role in my life.

After receiving my Master's degree in piano performance from The Juilliard School in New York City and two successive Fulbright Grants to Rome, Italy, I have had many wonderful opportunities to perform in grand concert Halls, including Carnegie Recital Hall in New York and Castel Sant' Angelo in Rome. In addition to performing, I have guided many talented pianists through intense technical and musical awareness. In 1996, I returned to my home in Macon, Georgia, to continue my performing and teaching career.

For a long time, I had a vision to establish a venue that would give other musicians and visual artists an opportunity to expand and share their talents. Opportunities to perform and exhibit works of art are not as numerous as one might think, and it is especially difficult if one expects to be reimbursed financially. Even those who support the arts might not understand why a talented person would spend a lifetime developing that talent at such great expense. The true artist must express the talent within—paid or not—and because of this, many are often taken advantage of by others.

Some of my earliest memories were of the happy and unforgettable times I spent in the home of my childhood neighbor, professional pianist Crockett Odom. I spent countless hours in his house, listening to him play his beloved Steinway grand piano. After a fire nearly destroyed it, I purchased it in 1999 with plans to restore it to its former glory and fill it once again with music. The house, which was built in 1906, rests on land originally owned by my great-great-grandparents, Adeline Woodruff and Samuel Insley Gustin and is on the same property where I grew up and where I live today. Samuel Gustin served as horticulturist and landscape architect for Central Park, and moved from New York City to Macon in 1863.

While the house was being restored, I was going through a restoration of my own: a series of painful spinal surgeries following a horrendous accident that almost destroyed my life and career. Returning home after a concert I had performed in 1996, my car was struck from behind by a tractor-trailer speeding over 100 mph. The injuries resulted in partial paralysis and atrophy of my right hand. Although I had to endure three years of physical therapy, I refused to let anything stop me from my dreams. Even while I was recuperating, I followed my vision and founded the Little Carnegie of the South in Crockett Odom's beautiful house. From the beginning, the idea of the new concert hall filled me with inspiration and promise. I always knew that it would become a reality. The process was gigantic, but never did I find it overwhelming. It has continued to grow from the very beginning and its success has gone beyond anything I could have ever imagined. Little Carnegie of the South has added an indescribable joy to my life and the lives of my children, Joseph Clisby White and Louise Logan White, now in their early 20s.

My dream didn't stop with opening the hall—after five years of not performing, I wanted to be the featured guest pianist for the opening concert. A courageous move, I admit, but I knew it wouldn't seem official to me if someone else debuted the hall. I scheduled three performances playing an extremely difficult repertoire, with a single plan in mind: the more difficult the music I chose to play, the harder I had to work to recover from the accident.

Little Carnegie of the South opened in 2003 amid much anticipation and excitement. Its intimate setting envelops the audience and allows the artists of every creative expression to share his or her talent with those who offer appreciation, encouragement and support.

My mother, Helen Clisby Barfield, was in her 90s when I completed the renovation, and she was in the audience the night of the grand opening. She always was my greatest supporter and the most gentle and loving mother anyone could ever have. She believed that any dream I had was always within my reach.

Besides the profound influence of my mother, world-renowned pianist and teacher Adele Marcus was the most inspiring musician I have ever known. Assistant for 12 years to the great pianist Joseph Lhevinne and a Juilliard faculty member until her death, Miss Marcus left me breathless by her playing, overwhelmed by her demands and exhausted by my attempts to reach the heights of her expectations. Spiritually, Mary Baker Eddy and her life-altering book *Science and Health With Key to the Scriptures* have expanded my consciousness into realms unimaginable.

I have always maintained that the right components merge and manifest themselves at the right time and, although difficult and challenging, the power and passion of thought can overcome any problem, setback or failure. I believe in the principle of perfection and an unlimited supply of energy and ideas. Focusing on these truths as the basis of our reality, anything is possible.

My advice to those who are in the fearful stage is to remember that fear will destroy your dream. Go forward, regardless, and strength will increase. Stop the suggestions of fear, and the answers will come. Always keep in mind that life is a process of unfoldment. Start with completeness, not lack or doubt. If one's motives are unselfish, the dream will develop a life of its own and all in its path will be blessed.

Chapter 9

WHY I TELL MY STORY

"God, grant me the serenity to accept the things I cannot
change, Courage to change the things I can,
And wisdom to know the difference."

– The Serenity Prayer

By "John Doe" & Nancy Irwin

I AM VERY FORTUNATE to have found a process to end my long history
of sexual activity with young boys. In gaining that approach, I know
it can succeed for anyone willing to accept responsibility, severely
self-evaluate and work diligently.

When I began meeting people—in group therapy sessions and
prison—who had been sexually victimized and saw the issues they

dealt with, I finally began to realize what my actions had been causing people in my life. When I was active, I would rationalize and minimize my sexual activities with young boys, not seeing the trauma I was causing in their lives. This realization was like a second education—and the most important one I ever gained. It began before I learned of the Sexual Disorders Clinic in Baltimore, Maryland.

Everything began falling into place at a mental health center in Kansas in the fall of 1983. I was 38 years old and facing a five-year prison sentence—my second conviction for the charge of indecent liberties with a minor. For nearly 20 years, I had lived the secret life of an out-of-control person attracted to young boys and the turmoil that goes with it. The progressive community was torn apart when I, one of its most prominent citizens, was charged with what it considered the most despicable offense imaginable.

That small Midwestern town had been a good turning point for me—a chance to start over after an initial conviction for my sexual offenses in in the early 1970s. I was paroled from a correctional facility after a nearly two-year sentence . I got a job with the town newspaper through a contact with the clinic and immediately began to develop a solid reputation. I was eventually offered the opportunity to purchase the newspaper and its print shop. I did so in 1976, and developed a staff that was producing one of the top publications in community journalism in the state.

I was beginning to put the pieces back together of what had been developing as a promising journalism career. I came from a well-educated family in Oklahoma; I had lived a good life and had all the makings of success. But there was a side to me that very few people knew about—and I didn't know where to turn.

The counseling I had received after my first incarceration had not specifically dealt with my sexual interest in adolescent boys and what that was all about. Like most clinics in the nation at that time, it had not identified the need for specific sexual disorder therapy. And thus, though the behavior modification process had been helpful on a short-term basis, it was only putting a "Band-Aid" on my thinking.

There were periods of time over the years when I did not engage in any inappropriate sexual activity at all. But I was waging an internal battle with myself; I had not come to grips with some major issues in my life that constantly simmered under the surface. Those who knew me well saw a volatile temper at times, a short fuse when pressured—especially in working with youth baseball teams. Seeking perfection in their performance, my anger surfaced many times. I later learned all those outlets were a way to let out a bit of the anger from the time bomb that was ticking inside.

A few weeks after my arrest in 1983, I was contacted by a man who had once coached baseball with me. He said he had taken time to decide whether he supported or condemned me. Having just experienced his son's drug rehabilitation therapy, he said he would be a hypocrite not to support me.

"I don't understand what you have done and what you are; I despise what you have done. But I sense you need help," he said during a visit. "I've liked you in all you have done besides this. I want to help." And with that statement, he handed me something his son had received—a medallion inscribed with the words of the Serenity Prayer. Little did I know the significance of those words at the time, but it was the beginning of what has become my relapse-prevention plan. It is the basis of every part of my life today. I carry that prayer with me everywhere I go.

After my arrest, I returned to those serene halls of the mental health clinic . The legal process had begun, as I had pled guilty to the charges. The clinic placed me in its treatment block for substance abuse to look at controls, and I was told to substitute my inappropriate sexual actions in place of drinking and drugs.

Amazingly, the two were similar. After making an emotional First Step presentation in one group following the 12 Steps process of serenity, some recovering alcoholic women told me how closely my story of pain and anguish followed their lives—that the actions were different, but the symptoms seemed the same.

My father sent me a copy of the book *Out of the Shadows* by Patrick Carnes. It explains the addictive sexual cycle, and as I read the book, I felt my life's story was being told in print. The book had just been published—no wonder we hadn't been able to pinpoint my behavior previously—it had never been publicized the way Dr. Carnes expressed it.

During this time , I had gained a close confidant in groups with a young lady from Ohio who had some problems while she was in school at the local state university. Much of it on the surface was based on her drinking problems, but it was far deeper. We identified closely—we liked sports and spent time playing basketball and talking. We became good friends; the therapy team seemed to grasp a bond between us and let us spend significant time together.

She was in the group the day I gave my First Step. One thing I hadn't shared with her was specifically why I was in the clinic. Well, she heard it all that day. And for the rest of the day, she was distant. She didn't sit with me at lunch and supper, which she always did. It concerned me greatly, because I cared for her. I asked my therapy assistant if I should go look for her. "No, give her time," he said. "She just heard some very difficult information about you. Let her have her space."

Each night before bed, this young lady and I always met in a day room and talked about how the day had been and anything else on our minds. Many times we went past curfew, but the staff always let us. On this evening, I entered that day room alone, still feeling naked to the world after my presentation earlier in the day. I sensed support from other fellow group members who had shared their appreciation for my honesty and willingness to talk about concerns they had in their own lives. Yet the one person from whom I wanted to hear was absent all day. And so I sat with my back to the rest of the room, lost in my thoughts, and working on a latch-hook rug project I had started at the clinic.

All of a sudden, I felt a tap on my shoulder, and my friend appeared and said, "Hey, want to talk?" A rush of emotion came over me like I can't describe. I learned someone could like and care for me, despite what I had done. I knew that I had tremendous support from family and friends, but this was a very special friend. Little did I know the significance of what I had said in my presentation. I was soon to find out as she and I talked over the next couple of days.

She shared how a relative had sexually abused her, and I began to see how those events affected her life. Her brother and some friends had violated her, she said, and it had left her with tremendous confusion. I can still recall the feeling, while hearing her story, of wanting to kill anyone who might hurt her.

I was beginning to understand the pain people felt from abuse.

Some close friends of mine saw Dr. Fred Berlin interviewed on the Phil Donohue television show, which was very popular at that time, and called me at the clinic to mention it. Dr. Berlin's treatment program at Johns Hopkins Hospital in Baltimore was doing some innovative work in the field of sexual abuse. My attorney contacted Berlin's office, and we were able to negotiate with the judge for my pre-sentence investigation to be an evaluation at Hopkins, at my cost.

That process didn't keep me out of prison, as we had hoped, but it did open the most important learning process of my life. I felt like a 500-pound weight was taken off my back as I attended my first group and was asked the most intimate, personal questions about my behavior that anyone had ever asked me before.

At the groups there, I suddenly found others were struggling with the same issues I was. It was a relief, and it was a safe climate that allowed me to open up and share what I had been holding in all my life. I found I wasn't alone, that other men have the same feelings, frustrations and actions. I heard some of them tell how their lives were unfolding several years after prison. Some even talked of gaining control over their deviant sexual urges before an arrest occurred.

Finally I began connecting the dots. Putting a face on the victim. Empathizing with these people—seeing their needs and respect, having candid conversations about our activities and feelings, being told we weren't bad people but were doing bad things that were hurting others and ourselves. I met other people who had been victimized and again began to empathize with their emotional pain, and related it to my own sexual activities.

Later on in my life, as I began my prison sentence in Kansas, I met a man in prison therapy who was serving a life sentence for killing his abuser. It was a very interesting story. The therapist had kept this man in individual therapy for a couple of years to work on the issues in his own life. This inmate had become "the prison punk"— usually the weakest man around, who becomes the sexual toy for any inmate's sexual gratification.

I learned later that he entered therapy to stop being a victim. And I can't think of a tougher environment to do that than in a prison. And so "the prison punk" stayed in individual therapy for a couple of years until our counselor decided it was time for him to join group therapy. I can see now that the therapist wanted this man to learn to face other offenders. But it was very important for me, and probably for some others in the group, to be able to just talk firsthand with someone who not only had been abused, but who literally had his life taken away because he acted out against his own perpetrators.

It was an eye-opening experience for me. There were many heated knock-down, drag-out discussions and arguments in that group, but I cherish those moments. I don't know where that gentleman is today, but I will always honor and respect him for what he meant to my recovery.

I was 43 years old when I was released from prison, and the most important steps since my prison days have been making acquaintances with numerous people who were victimized sexually. Listening as they describe the burdens they have carried and their difficult journeys to recovery has made me realize the impact of sexual abuse on a person. It keeps fueling my resolve to never offend again. At the top of the list is "Mary," whom I met in 1996. As we got to know one another, and learned of the many similarities in our paths to recovery, she helped me by showing me the need for victims and offenders to work together to stop sexual abuse. This is called restorative justice, and it is amazingly healing.

Today I live a successful wellness plan, which is a strategy to prevent relapse. I had parts of it in place in the past, but the most serious missing ingredient back then was that I didn't share specific issues with people close to me. I have found that I must have a core of people with whom I can openly talk about my feelings and resolve them.

Rather than being intimidated by my attraction to some teenage boys, I accept it, I acknowledge it; I do not dwell on it, and it does not control me. It was a very scary thing for me to accept. I remember filling out an insurance policy once, it required me to be specific about the issue I was treating. Depression wouldn't cut it; I had to put down the word pedophilia ... I didn't want to write or say that word.

But, today I *can* say that word, and its variations, like ephebophilia, which is the attraction to adolescents as opposed to pre-pubescent children. Just as I seek professional medical help for my vision (I have myopia; I'm near-sighted and have worn glasses since I was eight years old) so I can see clearly, I also seek professional help for my other health issue: I am an ephebophile. It's a much more serious one, for it affects a lot of other people. I found a psychological procedure that helps me control ephebophilia. It helps me gain an understanding of that behavior and how I can go through life controlling it for myself and not harming others. I've gained a strategy to cope with my feelings and fulfill my emotional and sexual needs consensually with age-appropriate partners.

I think one of the most important things that needs to be understood about sexual offenders is that there is a broad spectrum of our behaviors. I'm disgusted to be compared to Jesse Timmendequas, the man who killed Megan Kanka. He's a sociopath as well as a violent sexual predator and a pedophile. While I'm not defending my own or anyone else' sexual offenses or criminal activity, I'm not a violent man. I'm not a murderer. The Timmendequases of the world, fortunately, are an extremely low percentage of sex offender cases, and yet are now being used to set a standard for every person convicted of a sex offense. (Coincidentally, I know a man who served time with Jesse Timmendequas at Avenel, New Jersey. I saw this man shortly after his parole and he was furious to know that this man had been released. He told me the men in his prison group could not believe the guy was released. They knew from his approach to therapy that he would reoffend.)

I also want to promote the fact that I gained this control that I have and found continued recovery without the stringent laws and scrutiny hanging over my head, as is the case today. I was a participant in a clinic that made it quite clear that my actions were despicable and must stop, and yet I was always shown self-respect. Being in an environment where I was welcome to talk about my behavior openly and with others who were confronting the same issues, I experienced a comfort zone to talk about the most intimate issues in my life—something I had never felt free to do before. Without that intervention, I would most probably still be acting out. Like I said, I am very fortunate.

My life was totally out of control for a long, long time. When I learned a control process for my behavior, and went through all the steps at Dr. Berlin's clinic before serving hard time again, and then later came back there on parole after my prison experience, I found that it works. I'm now into my 24th year without abusing, after living more than 20 years totally out of control. I think that makes quite a statement about the power of proper treatment, and this is why I tell my story.

People are always asking me if I was ever sexually abused myself, as are a majority of molesters. I never was. One of the things that helped me explain my own sexual proclivity was an article I read at Johns Hopkins written by Dr. John Money, who co-founded the clinic with Dr. Berlin. The article stated that different types of trauma at a developmental stage of life can have a major impact.

There were some events in my life that occurred during my adolescence that were very, very difficult for me. Having moved a lot while growing up in an academic family, I was quite content in the 6th and 7th grade at a new place in Nebraska, where I was well received by the kids in my class. Geographical relocation can be very difficult for young people, and late in my 7th-grade year, I learned we would be moving again.

In discussions with my mother, I have pieced together that my behavior became very unmanageable after that news. I didn't want to go school or church, became quite rebellious and basically went into an introverted shell. All of this occurred, as I later recalled, when I was going through puberty. Solitary sports games became a huge part of my life and I isolated a lot from others. Masturbation also became a major recreation for me during this time, to the extent that I later could see how the addictive nature of sexual thoughts may have gotten a start.

I'm not saying that anyone who goes through adolescence ends up a pedophile or ephebophile. Most of us have had difficult issues or traumas to deal with in our youth, and yet most don't end up attracted to children or teens. As our culture struggles to find answers to the causes of this aberrant sexual attraction, I offer that it just so happened to occur this way for me.

I can tell you from personal experience in prison, in therapy, and now as an advocate, that a huge majority of the offenders I've met or communicated with express true remorse and have a serious desire to correct their behavior. The largest problem they face is the unavailability to a therapy approach like I had. The masses would rather believe that we are all untreatable … hopeless. But we've taken responsibility. We've taken ownership of what we've done. We're remorseful. We realize the pain we've caused other people. We are doing all we can to make sure it doesn't happen again.

I now make presentations and incorporate a dialogue with sexual abuse victims to show the importance of the entire picture being viewed for total restoration to occur. From October 1993 to June 2007, I directed Sex Offenders Restored through Treatment (SORT), one of several issue chapters of Citizens United for the Rehabilitation of Errants (CURE), a national organization that seeks to reduce crime through reform of the criminal justice system. SORT is a program that promotes prevention of sex abuse by those who previously acted out sexually inappropriately by participating in effective therapy. It pursues the use of alternative sentencing, when appropriate, that includes effective sex offender treatment. And it promotes the need for effective therapy in all correctional facilities for those incarcerated for a sex offense. I was a member of CURE's board of directors.

I also directed a non-profit organization, the Sex Abuse Treatment Alliance (SATA), from 1997 to 2007, after its founder and SORT's founder, Loren Perry, died. It is a coordinating organization assisting in bringing treatment providers in touch with each other, assisting in disseminating information of treatment for those who need it and coordinates education and public information programs that inform society about sex abuse, both from the perspective of victims and offenders. From 1996 to 2002, I was a member of the board of directors of Stop It Now!, a non-profit organization in Haydenville, Massachusetts, whose mission is to urge abusers and potential abusers to take ownership of their actions and responsibly seek help. It also educates the public on ways to stop sexual abuse and to increase public awareness of the trauma of child sexual abuse.

I, of all people, know that there are thousands of others out there like me who may feel lost, helpless, hopeless. Controlling inappropriate sexual behavior *is* possible. There is help. There *is* hope. And this is why I tell my story.

Chapter 10

WHAT IF...?

*"In a minute there is time for hundreds of decisions
and revisions which a minute will reverse."*

– T.S. Eliot

By Rabbi John Crites-Borak & Nancy Irwin

NOT ONLY HAVE I been through a series of career changes, but spiritual changes as well. I entered rabbinical school when I was 43; I went year-round in an accelerated program, took 12 semesters in four years and graduated in May 2000 as a Conservative rabbi. I trained in Zeigler Rabbinical Studies at the University of Judaism in Los Angeles. I was not born Jewish nor was I raised as a Jew. I started my career as an air traffic controller until the Professional Air Traffic

Controllers Association (PATCO) strike in 1981, when I lost my job. I had moved to the Midwest, but returned to LA after the strike, where I soon got a make-work job in the office of a different union. My job was to fill out membership forms for people recently hired in the industry. I soon realized the union leadership believed new members would automatically understand the need for—and the value of—the union. They had no answers for questions I heard every day. "Why do I have to join a union?", "What do I get in return for the money I'm paying the union?" and so on. I went to my boss and said, "What if I designed a seminar that could help people answer those questions?" He replied, "That's a fine idea, but how are we going to fund it?" I worked out a simple funding plan that my boss liked. We ended up earning just a little money, but a lot of good will.

At about the same time, I noticed that we had a newsletter. It was really ugly— brown ink on brown paper. Again, I went to my boss, "What if we did it this way?" and gave him a few ideas. He put his arm around me and said, "Congratulations! You're our new editor." This was in the early '80s, when people just started getting computers and everyone was learning Word Perfect, so I talked my boss into setting me up with equipment and software, and I redesigned the newsletter. The next thing you know, another union saw it and liked it and asked me to design their newsletter, then another union called, then another and another.

I started looking around and I thought, what if we merged all of our members—in this case 6,000 people—into a buying unit and got services? So I started shopping around and talking to possible vendors. I met with a marketing director from one law firm and asked, "In exchange for us directing all of our personal-injury business toward you, what would you be willing to do for our folks?" The marketing director said, "One day a week, we'll have an attorney in your office to provide your members a free half-hour consultation on any legal matter."

So we brought in a law firm and it just grew from that—we got travel discounts, Costco memberships and more. It all worked out very well, and later the marketing director and I got together and formed our own public relations and advertising firm. For the next 10 years or so, I was an ad/PR man focusing primarily on affiliate organizations and benefit providers. By the end of the 10 years, we were doing local and statewide ballot campaigns, national benefit programs for the AFL-CIO, making a good income and doing some good work.

Meanwhile, spiritually, I was at a loss. My own spiritual history was a little sketchy. My dad is a lapsed Catholic and my mother is a lapsed Protestant of some kind, and neither had been inside a church in my lifetime except for weddings and funerals. I wasn't raised in any sort of church at all, but one Sunday morning when I was 7, my father said, "Put on your good clothes, you're going somewhere." After changing, I got in the car and my dad drove me to the closest church in the neighborhood. He handed me two nickels, "One's for the collection plate," he said, "and you can buy a candy bar with the other one on the walk home."

This went on for a couple of years. I would get home around noon, my parents were at the kitchen table drinking coffee, my two older sisters would be doing the dishes and my breakfast would be petrifying in the oven. One day, I walked in, looked around and asked, "Why do I have to go to church when nobody else does?" I never went back.

I grew up knowing that I had so much potential, and my parents were unable to deal with it. I knew there was something for me in life; I just didn't know what it was.

When I was 15, I went to Mexico as part of a student exchange program. I lived with a family who didn't speak English, and I only had two years of high school Spanish, but we all got along. What was so interesting was they were devout Catholics, and my first Sunday there we all went to Mass. I walked in and was like, wow! The incense, the candles, the robes, the bells, the kneeling and the standing, the choir and the chanting, and it was just fabulous. I only had a very conservative Protestant experience—"Don't drink. Don't smoke. Don't play cards. Don't dance. Don't go to the movies. Don't, don't, don't. And by the way, folks, we're all made in God's image." My sense of God was, if we're all made in God's image, then God must certainly be uptight! But the

Mass was glorious. After the service, my host family and I went on a picnic. Every Sunday was the same. We went to Mass, then a picnic or a party at somebody's house.

That first Sunday, sitting at the other end of the picnic table was the priest, still in his collar, and I was stunned to see him sitting there with a cigarette in one hand and a big glass of red wine in the other. I remarked to someone, "He's a priest and he's drinking and smoking! How can he do that?" "What do you expect?" someone said. "He's only human." It was the first time I had ever connected religion with humanity. It was a real eye-opener for me. Then I started investigating religions.

When I got back to the United States, I went to the Christian Missionary Alliance, which is a radical Presbyterian fundamental offshoot; I was a Lutheran for a while; Baptist for a short time; a Buddhist for a year. I spent a year in *est*, a "transformational" self-improvement course that was popular in the '70s and '80s. I also participated in the Native American church on the Navajo Reservation for a while. It was all very interesting, but none of them were me. It's like putting on some new clothes, and they fit okay but when you look in the mirror, you realize they just don't feel right. And none of this felt right.

I ultimately decided that no religion was right for me. I would just be spiritual. Then when I hit 32, I happened to be listening to Dennis Prager, a syndicated radio talk show host, and somebody called in and asked, "Dennis, why should I be religious? Isn't it enough to be spiritual?" His answer led to me to where I am today. He said, "Because religion is to spirituality as language is to thinking. It gives us a way to organize, develop and express what goes on in our souls in a way that language does before it goes into our minds." I thought this was an intriguing idea. I decided to start looking at religion from that point of view.

My quest eventually led me to Catholicism. Even though I converted and was baptized, I knew there would be a problem—the theology never made sense to me. I constantly argued with and challenged the priest, but he could never fully answer all the questions I had. I hoped that if I prayed hard enough, I would have the epiphany and the revelation would grab me and I would finally BELIEVE. But it never happened.

The priest and I would go 'round and 'round on these questions I had. "It's just a matter of faith," the priest would say. "Father, how do I get faith?" "Pray," he said. But no matter how hard I prayed, I never got faith.

One Sunday we got into a really big argument. The next day, as I was getting my hair cut, I told my barber (who's Jewish) the story from church the day before. She took a step back and said, "John, I don't know why you put up with all that *mishigass*. You're the most Jewish man I know."

Judaism was one religion I hadn't tried.

When I got back home, I opened the phone book and started calling synagogues, "Hello, my name is John. I'm a Catholic. Somebody said Judaism might be a better fit for me. Can you tell me about it?" Rabbi Stewart Vogel of Temple Aliyah in Woodland Hills, California, answered my call. After I told him my story he said, "I have bad news. We don't have the answers. Don't get me wrong; we have lots of answers but not THE answer. But if you're looking for a place where you can ask life's most interesting, profound, meaningful, difficult kinds of questions, then maybe you'll find a home with us."

He recommended the Introduction to Judaism program at the University of Judaism [now the American Jewish University] in Los Angeles, and I enrolled. I did not intend to convert, just to explore. As I sat in the class, the more I heard and the more I studied, the more I found that it all made sense to me. So I converted.

And the more I learned about Judaism, the more I fell in love with it. One night, a couple of years after I converted, I was having dinner with my friend Rabbi Debra Orenstein. She asked me what I intended to do with all the knowledge I'd acquired. I hadn't given it much thought, but she suggested, "Why not be a rabbi?" I'm one of those people who firmly believes that if we listen, God will talk to us—maybe not directly, but God does talk.

That Saturday I went to synagogue. Toward the end of the service a little girl tugged at my pants leg and asked, "Are you a rabbi?" "No," I answered her. "Well, you look like a rabbi. You should *be* a rabbi." Was I getting a message from God?

Back when I was doing corporate consulting, I used to tell people, "If one person comes along and calls you a horse, well, that's interesting. If a second person comes along and calls you a horse, that's an amazing coincidence. But if a third person comes along and calls you a horse, my friend, it's time to get fitted for a saddle."

At the time, to be a Conservative rabbi you had to go to New York, where the only seminary in North America was. So I signed up and was accepted into the preliminary program, but when the time came for me to go, I said, "You know what? I can't go. I haven't had a crisis of faith yet." No relationship is mature until there's been a crisis; at least, that's what I believe. So I deferred for a year and went to Israel for a month, then to Europe to visit the concentration camps. During that year I went to every synagogue that I could because I wanted to find out two things: First of all, was I really Jewish or was this just another phase? Second, if I really was Jewish, where did I fit in?

By the end of the year, a lot of things happened. First, I had grown up next to a toxic waste dump and there was a class action suit—it cashed out and I got a big chunk of settlement money. Second, I didn't have to go all the way to the seminary in New York because one opened in Los Angeles. And third, I met a woman who fully supported my decision to be a rabbi. In fact, I told her on our first date of all my plans, and instead of saying, "Check, please" like most of my dates, she simply said, "That's great. What can I do to help you?" And now we've been married 11 years.

In my senior year of rabbinical school I actually adopted her last name as part of my family name. It was my way of acknowledging her and her family for their consistent and loving support. Crites is my last name and Borak is hers.

While I was considering becoming a rabbi I asked myself this question: at the end of my days, when I'm standing on my grave looking back, what did I want to be able to say about how I used this gift of life? Hmmm, let's see ... that I sold some products, got some people elected, made a lot of money and had a very easy life. Or that I helped people connect with what I believe is the most loving, nurturing, joyous way there is to live a life. I sold my business and, at the age of 43, entered the seminary.

Now I've started an educational foundation called *Amud ha-Shachar*/First Light. *Amud ha-Shachar* is the Talmudic phrase in Hebrew that refers to the very first hint of light in the eastern sky, long before the sun breaks the horizon. I am teaching modern men and women how to use traditional Judaism to bridge the gap between our everyday and our spiritual lives.

Toward the end of the introduction program, my class and I had a session at the Holocaust Museum here in LA and Lily Winter, a Holocaust survivor, spoke to us. Part of the conversion process is choosing a Hebrew name, so I asked her if it was all right if the Hebrew name I chose was a name of someone who was killed in one of the camps. Even though she said yes, I still checked with Rabbi Orenstein, who is the principal author and editor of *Lifecycles: Jewish Women on Life Passages & Personal Milestones*. Not only did she say it was absolutely fine, but that her family would be honored if I chose the name of one of her relatives who was killed.

I have to tell you, I was feeling pretty good about it. Once they heard the story, people thought it was a wonderful gesture on my part to take the name of someone who had died so tragically in a concentration camp. But I hadn't really thought about it beyond the good feelings it generated on my behalf.

The day came when I realized that I didn't know anything about the person whose name I was adopting. What if he wasn't religious? Did he spend his time in the synagogue or the coffeehouse? And who was I, after all, to be carrying around the name of this man who was murdered? I ultimately decided that I would live my life in such a way that no matter who my namesake was, people would be proud that I was around and that I was Jewish.

In this odd, unexpected way, it really helped me out, because later when I was faced with situations in which I wasn't sure which direction to take, the question became, which course of action would most likely bring the most honor to that name? A couple of years ago I had the opportunity to visit Auschwitz and say the *Mourner's Kaddish*, the traditional prayer for the dead, for him because I knew that was the only place in the entire world where our paths would cross.

The interesting thing about this is most Jews are named by their parents after people they loved and admired, so the question I like to teach is, "What's your Hebrew name? Why did your parents give you that name? What qualities and characteristics about that relative did they admire and hope that you would emulate? And in what ways can that name help guide you in this world?" And when I'm counseling expectant couples and I'm going to do a baby naming, one of the things I have the parents do is write a letter to their son or daughter explaining why they chose the name and what that person meant to them. And, at the baby naming, I have the parents read the letter or at least talk about it. Then at the child's *bar mitzvah* or *bat mitzvah*, read it and present it to the child. Or give it when he or she marries or has a commitment ceremony. This way the letter becomes an heirloom and helps guide them through their lives."

And that's what I've taken on—helping people discover the beauty of Judaism— and to help them learn skills so they can teach it to their family and friends in a way that says, "There is value in being Jewish besides the chicken soup." I conduct workshops and seminars across the country, and everything's falling into place. I'm more convinced than ever that if we listen to God's voice—whether we call it intuition or coincidence or universal energy—it will take us where we need to go. And the courage doesn't lie in determining what the future will be; it lies in the faith that we were created for a purpose. Our job is to fulfill that purpose, even if day by day we don't know exactly what it's going to be.

Chapter 11

THE BEST LAID PLANS

"The definition of hope is the confident expectation of good."

– Anonymous

By Leslie Buterin Brown & Nancy Irwin

I HAVE BEEN FORTUNATE to live an abundant life, full of health, career, and relationship valleys and peaks. And in the past decade or two my life has been filled with great hope. Hope being the *confident expectation* of good.

For over 35 years, I was plagued with a multitude of inexplicable health problems and a laundry list of puzzling symptoms: exhaustion after exercise that required a ten day recovery period; shooting pains, feelings of bugs crawling under my skin; dizziness, oh-the-itching that lotion could not soothe; and dozens more symptoms. Physician after physician concluded the "illness" was all-in-my-head. They believed each and everyone of my symptoms to be psychosomatic.

Life goes on and so did I trying to convince myself those doctors were right even though my symptoms grew worse. In 1979 after receiving my Master's in Business Administration from the University of Kansas, Amoco Oil Company moved me to their Chicago Headquarters as an Equal Employment Opportunity Consultant. I traveled all over the country making sure our Amoco Production Company's facilities were in compliance with Federal Regulations.

Within a few years I was offered a position with Harris Bank. I accepted in hopes of staying in Chicago and finding wellness. I left that position as the "all-in-my-head" symptoms sent me to bed for two years.

As energy slowly returned, I focused on doing things that gave me joy. Such as baking my grandmother's banana bread. Seemed fitting, as all my life I had said, "My last name is Buterin, like butterin' bread. In a casual conversation with the owner of the neighborhood grocery he said he would be glad to sell whatever baked goods I brought him and that's how "Mother Buterin's Baked Goods" began.

Another change was in store for me as I was invited to sell fine art. The commissions on $2,000 to $30,000 artworks were considerably larger than the margins on my banana bread at the time and I loved being around people so I accepted. Earning a living on full commission sales laid the foundation for the sales knowledge I now use for my current, longstanding, sales consulting business.

Travels took me to interesting parts of the world, but when my grandfather died, my mother died, and my grandmother died. I began wondering is life all about making decisions based on more money, more prestige, and more opportunities for advancement. I hoped not, as life led that way was leaving me feeling empty. I left my position as Gallery Director and thought about these things.

June 18, 1991 after a four-hour Bible-centered conversation with my friend and sales mentor, Anna, she spoke words that changed my life forever. "You are so close to the Lord in your thinking, what keeps you from giving your life to him?"

I had no intellectual understanding of what she was asking me. But my spirit understood. I had a picture in my mind of a red-brick wall with white-chalk writing. I literally "read the writing on the wall" and replied, "my anger."

As I read/said those words, I was washed from the top of my head to the bottom of my feet in warm relaxation. All of the tension, anger, unforgiveness, and general yuckiness left my body. Overnight I was changed. It took three months before I understood that I had been born again in Christ. I was giddy with joy as I made amends with people I had hurt and those who had hurt me. I had a voracious appetite for scripture and read the Bible cover-to-cover two times in one year.

All sorts of new friends from different walks of life came into my life as I joined Bible study groups. One friend said, "Les, you can love the Lord but you still need income. How about taking a temp job doing cold calls to prospects for my dad's company until you figure out your next career path?"

Little did I know, her dad's company was a half-billion-dollar company that he wanted to take to a full-billion-dollar company using the very job that I was invited to do. That temp job launched the sales consulting practice I have today, TheTopDog.com. But, I'm getting ahead of myself.

The Lord had a big job to do. He helped me grow up emotionally and rebuilt my character on a rock-solid foundation on which my new God-honoring life could be built.

I had many exhausting, self-defeating beliefs to overcome, such as:

- **If I was good at something, then it must have no value.**
  Wrong-o. Being good at something is an indication the skills I have are a good fit with the task at hand.
- **My work must be perfect before moving forward. I am far from being perfect; therefore, I must not move forward.**

No way. Life is a process; imperfections make us interesting and allow us to team up with others who can compensate for our weaknesses by using their strengths

- **A little bit of success is irrelevant.**

  In fact, a little bit of success is proof that something can be done.
- **Failure at a task means I am a failure as a person.**

  Nope. Failures actually serve to keep us on track for success. Failure is great feedback that there is something to learn that will help me get back on course. There are always new adventures in growth to be had.

Then I had a laundry list of fears to overcome:

- Fear of success
- Fear of failure
- Fear of what others would think about me
- Fear of not pleasing others, even to the point of fearing making others look foolish if they thought I couldn't accomplish my goal and I actually did!

Talk about a false belief system that produced emotional paralysis ... sheesh! As my thoughts were put into order, I could better see the obstacles that I wanted to overcome:

- **Emotional obstacles:** I had gone down the path of feeling victimized at every turn, I wanted to feel ready to handle anything and to feel victorious.
- **Spiritual obstacles:** I lived a worldly life driven by fear and made decisions by running from what I did not want. My new goal was to live a God-honoring life and to make decisions by moving toward what I did want.
- **Physical obstacles:** I lived with chronic illness and I wanted vibrant health.

The more involved I became in applying Bible-based principles in my life, the more opportunities came my way. I was invited to do a regular "organizing your home and office" segment on a TV station and speak throughout the state of Illinois to give my conversion testimony.

Then, about 9 months later, I felt an emotional hole open up in my heart—the size of the Grand Canyon. I wanted more than anything to be back in Kansas City near my little nieces, my sister and the rest of my family. Odd, since family had been a source of great emotional pain for me. But I missed them all, so I moved.

While scouting out Kansas City I began looking for a church but none of the churches I visited seemed to be a fit for me. I pulled over onto the shoulder of the interstate and cried. "Lord, I know you are all about restored relationships. I am glad to move back even though there is so much emotional pain for me here. But could you please direct me to a good church?"

The next place I visited had seven people attending on a Wednesday night, and I knew I had found a church home even though they were without leadership at the time. I moved on Monday. By Wednesday, I was on the way out of town for a women's ministries retreat. I went on to teach classes on Sunday mornings.

Within a year, a senior pastor was elected. He invited me to serve on staff as single pastor with people ages 18 to 81. Shortly after that, the pastor created a new position called "corporate ministries pastor." Serving in that role, I traveled the country to corporate America and conducted sales training. I always took one of the young women in singles ministry with me as my assistant and as an apprentice of sorts. Every time we were on the road, people approached us to discuss their spiritual concerns. Manicurists, limousine drivers, sales professionals and executives alike—all were spiritually hungry, and we were honored to be there with them and for them. The church grew and continues to grow exponentially.

Family relationships have been restored, and we are each a mutual source of comfort for the others. I am incredibly thankful for the unwavering support of friends, family and a Godly husband, who is a tremendous source of encouragement, wise counsel and love.

In May of 2003, I quite by "accident" went to a physician who listened to me and gave an accurate diagnosis for my list of the more than 150 symptoms that interrupted my health. Turns out for over

35 years, Lyme disease—multiple infections in the brain—had been the source of my health problems. All caused by a bite from a little tick no bigger than the head of a pin. I cried with relief that I was right, that something was terribly wrong. And I laughed, thinking, those doctors were right—it was all in my head! The infections were all in my brain.

The treatment process is quite involved and for me took five years. Lyme is bacteria. Antibiotics get rid of bacteria. Lyme also travels with co-infections; the ones I have are viral. Viruses don't go away, but the body can strengthen to the point where the viruses go dormant and do no harm. Today I am thankful to be well and living a productive life.

The Lord says in the book of Isaiah, "I will bring beauty out of the ashes." He is true to his word. My health experiences and those of my husband—who had been misdiagnosed as having Crohn's disease which was in reality Lyme disease—have been committed to writing. We are helping people from all over the world to get their lives back and to regain excellent health through our website TheLymeLady.com.

What can you take from my life experiences to make your life even better? I'll try to summarize what I have learned and hold onto.

- **Take God seriously.** Whether you believe it or not, I know there is a God who sent his only son to die for you. Get to know him.
- **Fear not.** God says, "Fear not." A life founded on that emotion is an exhausting life spent in a state of survival-only, like treading water 24/7. On the other side of fear(s) is freedom to live life abundantly. Do what you need to do to let loose of fear.
- **Have hope.** Hope is the confident expectation of good. As it is written in the book of Jeremiah, "For I know the plans I have for you, says the Lord, plans to prosper you not to harm you, plans for hope and a future."

My *hope* is that you too learn to live life to its fullest, as life is quite a marvelous gift.

Chapter 12

COUNSELOR, HEAL THYSELF

"Things happen for a reason."

– Unknown

By Gary Gwilliam, Esq.

A S THE CHILD, GRANDCHILD, and great-grandchild of alcoholics on both sides of my family, I was 11 times more likely to be alcoholic than the average person. For a long time, I was able to convince myself my drinking was under control because I was too smart, too successful and never drank at lunch during a trial. Unlike some alcoholic attorneys I knew, I didn't keep a bottle at work, and I didn't start drinking until after the workday was done.

By my mid-40s, however, I had started to admit that my drinking was seriously damaging my body, my marriage and my relationship with my daughters. I had cut down on drinking and substituted wine for scotch. I also started therapy with a doctor who was concerned about my liver if I didn't stop drinking and delirium tremens if I stopped cold turkey. Yet I was lying to the therapist, so the therapy wasn't working.

When my wife Liz made a date for us in June 1984, I thought we were going out for dinner and drinks with another couple. Instead, she led me to a booth in a coffee shop, where three attorneys and a stranger were sitting.

She told me they were there to talk to me about drinking ... and I thought that meant they wanted to have a drink. I blew up when instead they said they were concerned for me and were there to help me get into a program to quit drinking. It was something called an intervention.

Before I angrily stomped out of the room, I demanded to know what right they had to talk to me about drinking. Was any of them a better lawyer than I? No one could or would say he was.

Sometime during the stonily silent drive home, I turned to my wife and said, "Well, you don't expect me not to have a drink after a thing like that, do you?"

Two scotches later, I still felt humiliated, but my deflated ego had to admit that the only person I was kidding about my drinking was myself. It was also obvious that Liz was on the verge of leaving me.

After an hour or so, I went to the room where Liz sat, crying softly. I told her I did not want her to leave, and that starting the next day, I would quit drinking. This was the first time I had ever made such a vow, and she decided to give me another chance. A week later, we took off for a vacation to Hawaii, which was the first vacation in my life where I had nothing to drink. It was wonderful.

The intervention was about joining an Alcoholics Anonymous program or going to a rehab center. Though I strongly support AA, especially the Other Bar for alcoholic attorneys, I made a different choice. I wanted to maintain sobriety on my own. I vowed, "I am never going to get in trouble with drinking again. I will live instead of dying." Except for one day and night many years ago, I have kept that vow.

Before I quit drinking, I had been unable to imagine life without alcohol. I've always been a very social person, and since high school, alcohol had been a key part of parties, playing cards, sporting events and every other fun event. If I gave up alcohol, how could I ever have fun in my life?

I soon discovered that nobody cared what was in my glass. Not only could I stay sober and enjoy being with others who drank, but I could also remember the event.

Eventually, Liz and I respectfully went our separate ways. When she died some years afterward, I spoke lovingly at her funeral.

Instead of drinking, I went to therapy and read. Dennis Wholley's book *The Courage to Change: Personal Conversations about Alcoholism* provided inspired stories by famous people who had overcome alcoholism. I read hundreds of other books, many on spirituality, which created a new foundation for a rich life.

I've always loved being a lawyer, and I've always had an impressive track record in my field—even during the many years when I was rarely sober in the evenings after work.

Spirituality changed the way I practice law. I still prepare logically for trial, but now I also meditate throughout the process. Simple breathing exercises help me keep centered, relaxed and focused on my client's needs without getting sidetracked by the other side's comments. I let go of obsessions about the past and worry for the future. I concentrate on the now.

One of the biggest lessons I learned is to stop being afraid of losing or showing vulnerability. For a lawyer, this is a huge deal, because we are trained to look tough all the time, and it's very hard not to take losses personally.

When my mother died suddenly in March 1998, I was in the midst of a difficult trial. Shortly after that, we lost that case. Instead of blaming myself and feeling ashamed as I had so often previously done, I reflected on the loss and what I had learned and gained while going through it.

I decided to write an article about how lawyers deal with their losses. Such an article, to my knowledge, had never been written, because lawyers don't like to talk about losing.

The article was published in national and state law journals. Many people were touched by it and gave me positive feedback. They appreciated that someone was willing to write about how we deal with the pain of losing and why it is important to us.

I also began to speak publicly with lawyers about my alcoholism and what I had done to overcome it. Although I was never active in AA, I was invited to a special candlelight meeting for trial lawyers in recovery. A good friend was there with a woman who sat quietly through the ceremony. I assumed they were dating.

I was the last to speak about all the good that had happened to me after I had quit drinking: better verdicts, improved relationships with clients, my work with other trial lawyers to overcome drinking, and the obsession with overwork or fear of losing. I also talked about my relationship with Liz, and how our eventual parting was very difficult but done with integrity.

When I was finished, the mysterious woman told me she appreciated my honesty, and that she had also left a marriage because it was the right thing to do.

Later I learned that the woman's name was Lilly. As she drove back to her home in Los Angeles, she felt both a strong impulse to call me but had ambivalence about calling an alcoholic man just coming off his second marriage.

Although Lilly had never called a man before in her life, she decided to call me. We made a date, and she drove from Los Angeles to Oakland to be with me. We fell in love, eventually married, and are real soul mates.

At 70, I still love preparing and trying cases, though I am shifting more into a mentor than active litigator role. Lilly and I travel a lot. As I write this, we are preparing to go to Machu Picchu and Antarctica.

Grandchildren are a special blessing. Although I never had a grandfather, I've learned how to be one by regressing with the kids and seeing the world through their eyes.

What would I say to someone else who wants to quit drinking, get off the gotta-win treadmill and have a soul mate? Actually, I had so much to say that I wrote a book, *Getting a Winning Verdict in My Personal Life: A Trial Lawyer Finds His Soul* (Pavior Publishing, 2007). It's been exciting to see the book's impact on other lawyers, several of whom told me the book helped them gain the courage to stop drinking.

Obviously, there's no substitute for the whole story in my book! But here's the essence: dare to face whatever is hard for you. Make a solemn vow to live your best life, then follow that with whatever spiritual guidance and human support works best for you. Maintain your integrity and always be open to a good surprise.

Chapter 13

NEVER SAY NEVER

"A life lived in fear is a life half lived."
– Proverb

By "Jane Doe" & Nancy Irwin

I F SOMEONE HAD TOLD me I was a lesbian, I would have laughed in their face. Growing up in a middle-class, extremely conservative town, I never in my wildest dreams would have thought I may be gay. I was raised a strict Catholic, so you can imagine what we were taught about any sexual expression outside of marriage, much less homosexuality! Looking back, I never really had any crushes or attraction to women.

I was extremely fortunate in that my parents were avid readers and proponents of higher education. Both encouraged me to be whatever I wanted and get the best college education possible. My mother, especially, really wanted me to have my own career, my own money and my own success before I got married. I myself wanted all those things, including a responsible man to settle down with one day and have children. And my life did follow that path, at first. I got married in my late 20s—though I insisted on keeping my own last name—and had four children, who are now teenagers and absolutely the lights of my life. They are worth every bit of the marital suffering I soon came to endure.

Around 39 years old, I began to wake up to the unhappiness I'd felt for a long, long time but denied. It was rather easy to overlook, as my professional life was soaring. I had (and still have) my own extremely successful business. My company received numerous prestigious awards, and somehow I found a way to balance being a mommy in there, too. Several factors played into my personal life wake-up call. For one, my mother was diagnosed with a terminal illness at age 58! She had always been my best friend, confidante, my foundation and my strength. Emotionally, this was a very lonely, difficult and isolating time for me. Although she was still married to my father, I assumed full responsibility and power of attorney for her. I suppose this slow, draining illness underscored the brevity of life for me, and I began to really be in touch with my unfulfilling and unhappy marriage. My husband was a raging monster and refused to seek professional help. His father was bipolar and, as one of almost a dozen children, nearly all of his siblings had similar behavioral problems.

After ignoring the warning signs for years, I experienced a defining moment one Sunday morning, when I knew with blinding clarity that I had to get out of there. I had been awake with our four young kids for about five hours while my husband slept in, and I decided to move his Jaguar (which I had bought him) from the garage to the front of the house so our kids wouldn't scratch his car while playing in the garage rec room. Unfortunately, the sprinkler system went off and got his car wet—which sent him into an unbelievably frightening rage upon waking up. That was the final straw for me. I knew that I so deserved to be treated better, that I could no longer subject my children to this man's erratic and damaging behavior and, most of all, that I needed and wanted to be happy again.

I filed for divorce. Though I was no longer a practicing Catholic, those early beliefs about divorce had apparently laid a very inflexible and unforgiving guilt system deep down in my psyche. It was excruciatingly difficult dealing with that guilt, four children in tow, my business ... and to cap it all off, I was falling in love with a woman. Was it really possible for me to have been heterosexual all my life and then find myself drawn to and deeply adoring a woman at age 40? I read as many books as I could and underwent therapy every week to deal with my double dose of guilt: divorce and homosexuality. And the confusion! I tried to get in touch with who I really was. Was I a straight woman who just happened to fall in love with a woman? Was this my truth? What personal strengths and weaknesses could help me or hinder me? In the end, I chose love. I decided to come out and be happy instead of suffering as someone I was not. And I knew I had the strength to stand up for the truth of my conviction.

While I felt enormous relief after making that choice, I still had fears to overcome. I was moving in a radically different direction, to say the least, and had virtually no support system—friends and family abandoned me, and I was the scandal of our neighborhood. It was an extremely isolating, challenging time for me, but what kept me going was my dedication to my children and my desire to find honest, authentic love and happiness. I wanted to model that for my children. Something switched in me, and when I finally did give myself over to being in love with a woman, my truth was so evident. It was an awakening that changed everything for me. Being loved by a woman was amazing, rich, fulfilling, irresistible and downright fun. The innate kindness and gentleness that a woman has is so very different from what I experienced with men.

If I had it to do all over again, I absolutely would. It was really the only way I could learn the invaluable lesson of staying true to myself and being honest and authentic. It was my journey, and definitely, definitely has had a happy ending. I learned that fear is no match for choosing happiness over suffering. When you are a parent, it's always better to take your children out of an unhappy situation and try to give them a better world. That first step is terrifying, but never look back, never regret. Getting there may be difficult, but it's so worth it. I am now in the most amazing relationship with a woman. It is everything I ever dreamed a loving and caring relationship could be. I am respected instead of disrespected, I am put first instead of last and I feel deeply loved for who I am—not what someone wants me to be. Making love is truly an awe-inspiring experience instead of a tedious one-way duty.

We all only pass this way once. Why waste even a minute of it being uncherished, unloved, unappreciated?

Chapter 14

PAY ATTENTION, YOUR LIFE IS CALLING

"There are two types of change: the change we choose,
and the change that chooses us."

– Linda Ellerbee

By Moira Shepard & Nancy Irwin

WHEN YOU'RE IN A midlife crisis and your soul is calling out to you, you better listen. Ignore it and it'll kick you right in the rear; or in my case, in the lower back.

Ever had that feeling that something's going to happen but you didn't know what? Or a feeling that you should go this way but instead you go that way? That's your intuition telling you to pay attention.

I was an office manager of a major magazine publishing company for 10 years, and I knew it was all wrong for me but couldn't bring myself to leave. Previously, I'd been an award-winning journalist (the paper's corporate owner closed it), an actress, novelist, columnist, publicist, bartender, bookkeeper, statistical researcher and even a mime. I knew I was unhappy with the way my life was going, but I chose to ride the wave of complacency. Then one day I bent over to pick up a 50-pound box of magazines and I felt a little crackle in my spine. It left me paralyzed for four years and bedridden for another three.

In Bed Forever?

I underwent five unsuccessful surgeries and nearly died when a blood clot formed on the left side of my body. You have a lot of time to think about your life under circumstances like that. At age 46, I thought, "What am I going to do? Just stay in bed FOREVER?!"

Sensing there was a larger purpose behind the events that laid me up for so many years, I just kept going, trusting I would discover the reason someday. The path I was to take became blindingly clear when I woke up at 4:30 in the morning on November 20, 2004. I sat up, suddenly wide-awake, knowing I had to start a worldwide organization to guide people in using their illness, injury and pain as a springboard to transformation. I knew I'd have to get well to carry out this vision. It took 18 months to get back on my feet again, but I did it.

The lower back pain has disappeared and my life has been transformed into one of contribution and fulfillment on a level I never dreamed possible.

Creating a New Life

Then, mindful of that 4:30 wake-up call, I turned my attention toward helping others. I've produced and hosted two motivational radio shows and am planning a third. I'm a certified Advanced ThetaHealing™ Practitioner and licensed ThetaHealing instructor. I've earned a certificate as a master practitioner and trainer in Neuro-Linguistic Programming (NLP), which is hypnotherapy and neurological re-patterning. And I'm a charter member of the International Board for Accelerated Human Change.

My mission is to empower people to channel intuition and self-trust to take control of their lives, create financial freedom, connect to inner wisdom, learn how to enjoy life again and more. The 4:30AM vision I had kept me going through all the self-doubt I experienced. It lit a fire in me that just gets stronger as time goes on. I was literally stopped from getting out of bed because I feared returning to my safe, "little" life. But to be of service—for that, I could get out of bed! I consecrated my life that day to following the vision. There is no Plan B.

A Few Technical Problems

First, I had to overcome my fear of public speaking. I also feared my physical strength wasn't sufficient for all the travel and training required by the mission. More important, I feared I would be laughed at.

I also had to overcome self-doubt, dependency on medication, and my inability to sit or stand more than 10 minutes a day. Plus, I was completely ignorant of how to start a business. But these were just minor problems for which I quickly found solutions. You just figure out these things as you go along.

What Makes it All Worthwhile?

Seven years is a very small price to pay for the life I have now. For one thing, I would never have learned the lessons I want to share with you:

1.   Let go of the past. Release grudges, resentments, and beliefs that no longer serve you.

2. Learn to live in the present and value who you are and where you are right now.

3. Develop a big-picture vision of the future you most desire—one that really lights you up.

4. Commit to following that vision; knowing it may change, and that you can roll with it.

5. Do what you do with love, or don't do it at all.

Finally, and most importantly, choose to trust yourself. Trust is more than an emotion—it's a decision, like love. Choose to trust, just for the next 30 seconds, that you know what you're doing. Choose to trust for another 30 seconds ... work up to five minutes a day. This builds your Trust Muscle. Eventually, it becomes your normal state of being. After that, nothing can stop you!

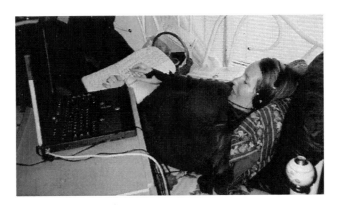

Chapter 15

FROM REEL LIFE TO REAL ESTATE

"Mind your own business."
– Robert Kiyosaki

By Ed Kramer & Nancy Irwin

I SPENT 25 YEARS as a computer graphics artist—including 12 as senior technical director and sequence supervisor at a well-known visual effects production company. Then I was laid off. But I'm very happy and grateful that I got to work on more than 20 blockbuster movies, where I supervised such effects as the scarabs in *The Mummy* and *The Mummy Returns* and the rock monster from *Galaxy Quest*.

A colleague of mine was getting laid off at the same time, and as we sat around reminiscing and discussing our post-laid-off plans, he shared with me information regarding how he managed his finances; I was impressed with all his business ventures. And this wasn't the stock market—these were investments in businesses and real estate that were returning income to his family on a passive basis.

I wanted to learn more. He recommended some books to me, and I went right out and bought *Rich Dad, Poor Dad*, the classic explanation of how "wealth" works, by Robert Kiyosaki. I read it cover to cover and that book was a real eye-opening experience for me. It convinced me that the best thing I could do after the layoff was to go into business for myself. Basically I had been making all of my bosses rich for my whole career, but now it was time to focus on doing it for myself.

Once I read the first of Kiyosaki's books, I read many of his other titles in the "Rich Dad" series, and I also started reading other classic books about business. For about six months, I attended seminars at the local Small Business Development Center, which covered topics such as "Writing a Business Plan" and "Financing for Start-Up Businesses."

Once the initial "yeah, I'm gonna be rich!" enthusiasm wore off, the negative thoughts started creeping in (and I still find myself trying to overcome them every day). You know, the typical "get a job with benefits and a paycheck every two weeks" instead of "build a business" thoughts. This is especially true since I have a wife, two kids and a mortgage.

But I also started having self-doubts about my ability to make it in today's marketplace as a computer graphics artist, even though I had built a top-notch portfolio over the years. I had been in the industry for so long and had watched it grow at an astounding rate, and these days literally thousands of new graduates enter the marketplace, willing to work for much lower salaries to get their foot in the industry's door. Also, since I had worked with proprietary software for so long, now there was a whole new generation of software I needed to learn to survive in today's marketplace.

After the layoff, I worked on a freelance job at another company doing visual effects for movies. Many of my friends were there as well, either from current or previous layoffs. I realized I could have made it as a freelancer, bouncing from company to company in the Bay Area, but it would have been difficult coming up with the Marin County mortgage every month.

With the real estate market threatening to start on a downhill slide, my wife and I decided that the best way to actually get ahead financially was to sell our lovely house on the water in Marin and to leave California for someplace where the monthly nut wasn't as big. My wife took on the task of looking around for the ideal environment for us, and we settled on a community south of Denver, Colorado. We couldn't be happier with our decision, and it also creates a bit of the "big fish in a small pond" feeling to the independent computer graphics art career I'm starting here.

I've always had regular paychecks and benefits, but now I'm spending my time, without pay, building relationships. I'm betting that one day soon this risk will be worth the reward of a much higher ultimate level of income. After the kind of career success I've already achieved, there's no reason to believe I can't crank it up a notch to a new level of success in the next 10 years. I've already made my plans and have a much better idea how to provide for my family's future. Once I'm finally making money again, I'll use that income in a much better way and set up the kinds of passive wealth through investments I learned about from my friend.

I have another bit of advice for you about managing your career. When I felt I was ready to move up to the next level and become a supervisor, I found success by aggressively courting the producers and managers who made such decisions. But over the years, many of my biggest fans and supporters left the company for various reasons. Resting on my reputation, I wasn't as aggressive about courting the new generation of decision-makers, and eventually I was not being requested as much for supervisory roles. My advice is to never to stop being aggressive about self-promotion, and to remain vigilant about staying up-to-date with the newest generation of movers and shakers in your company/field.

Luckily, I've always been able to depend on my wife, Kim, for support. She's great about taking care of the reality of day-to-day living, seeing to it that the bills get paid, the kids get to school and the family runs smoothly so I can focus on the business I'm trying to get up and running. She's also great to bounce ideas off of and for advice (which I often take) about getting along in this new business world. She's also my social director, and sees to it that we make time to go out with friends and to have date nights with each other.

My new business is building. I have now incorporated and partnered with a well-established visual effects and editing facility in Denver, called !mpossible Pictures. Through networking, I have managed to bring in a production for a major network, providing the high-end graphics for an amazing show scheduled to air in 2008. They liked the idea that I was outside of the California marketplace and could assemble a team specifically for their project. Now I am bidding on the visual-effects contract for a multi-million-dollar feature film, reading scripts, networking in the local filmmaking community and gearing my visual-effects business for more movies and major network television.

I have a number of heroes whose love and commitment to what they do keep me going. I love baseball, and when I was a kid, my dad would take me to see Hank Aaron. Now that I'm older, and I realize what his playing time was all about, I'm even more in awe of his accomplishments. In my own field, many of the people who used to be my heroes have since become my friends. I've actually gotten to work with many of the visual-effects pioneers in my industry, including Dennis Muren (with his **six** Visual Effects Oscars!), Douglas Trumbull (who created the visual effects for *2001: A Space Odyssey*), Carl Sagan, and Friz Freleng (animator who invented Bugs Bunny and Wile E. Coyote).

If you have a financial dream to pursue, start your education by reading books about wealth creation. I like Kiyosaki, but there are plenty of other authors with similar ideas. Consider taking the skills you've learned over the past years and starting your own business. Call all your old friends and clients—they're all older now too, and many of them have probably done the same thing. They may very well need your services, or the services of the team you can put together. You may have to struggle with the idea of not getting a regular paycheck. And benefits are outrageously expensive when they aren't provided by an employer—get politically active in the issue of universal health care.

And, of course, read books like this one for the psychological need to relate to others in the same boat. If all you've ever done with your savings is to invest in stocks and mutual funds, there's a much bigger and better way for you to go. Just get started and take action.

Photo: Noah Berger

DR. IRWIN'S SELF-HELP TIPS FOR WHEN LIFE BLINDSIDES YOU:

1. Give yourself full permission to freak out! Maybe not in front of the boss who just laid you off, but as soon as humanly possible. Call a loved one and get to a safe setting and allow yourself to scream, cry, rant, rave and release all the natural negative feelings you have every right to feel. Life might demand you put these feelings on hold (children, work, etc.), but schedule in time every day to get in touch with your feelings. This will allow you to control those feelings, instead of getting further blindsided. You are in a situation that you cannot control, but remember that you can control your response to the situation. This process may take weeks or months. Honor your own pace. Like grieving, it can come and go. Expect that, and prepare for it. It is perfectly natural.

2. If you are spiritual, go to a church or synagogue or mosque or temple when there is no scheduled service. We tend to get caught up in the social etiquette during scheduled formal services, so give yourself time alone with your faith. If you are not spiritual, go to your favorite natural setting. A walk or rest on a beach, through a forest, by a lake, etc., can allow you to honor your own spirit. Nature can literally and metaphorically ground you. Go at your favorite time of day. Take a journal and just purge all your feelings.

3. Just as Mother Nature is naturally healing, so are pets and children. The innocent, pure unconditional loving energy of animals is therapeutic for most people. So are gardening, painting, writing— anything with the earth or creative arts connects you to the earth, to others, to your higher self.

4. Do something frivolous. It may be buying yourself a dozen roses or having a massage. It is crucial (and does not have to be extravagant!) to send an expression to your soul that you are on your side. You've just received devastating news; soften that blow in any way you can.

5. Eat healthy foods and stay hydrated. Even if you have no appetite due to your anguish, eat what you can. You are in fight-flight mode and need to return to normal as quickly as possible. Try to eat

even a small amount of something calming (high proteins, fresh fruits, vegetables). It is important to normalize your body and your routine as quickly as possible.

6. Set your alarm and get up at your usual time. Even if you have been fired, your new job is looking for a new job, and you want to continue sending the message to your body and mind that you are working. Keeping normal hours and routines will keep you in your normal rhythm. You might be tempted to wallow in the bed (and in self-pity!), so give yourself a set number of days to do just that. Put a time limit on it, and then back to normal. Keeping status quo will give you a feeling of being in control.

7. Get physical exercise. You need the endorphin release now more than ever. It won't make your problem go away, but you will get a fresh perspective on it and renew your positivity. No one ever felt worse after working out.

8. Close your eyes and imagine you can write a happy ending for this challenge. In her wonderfully inspiring book: *Write it Down: Make it Happen*, Dr. Henriette Anne Klauser illustrates the ease of manifesting your vision. It may sound crazy, but even if you've been diagnosed with a disease, write down that you are healing. Remember, your thoughts are directions for your subconscious. Feel any fear or anger, yet focus on healing. Allow yourself to write out several endings for your predicament from sublime (I win the Lotto) to ridiculous (space aliens abduct me so I won't need to find a new job). This allows you cut through the fear with some humor and move to a realistic solution and appropriate actions. (I go on several job interviews and nail one that is way better than the one I just lost) and then write out and begin taking the action steps to create that in reality.

9. Find at least one person who has survived what you are now experiencing. No matter what befalls you, you are not the first, nor the last. None of us is alone. There is great comfort in sharing negative experiences. Make sure you don't get sucked into a negative, victimy "Life sucks" vortex. Focus on the way out, around

or through the negative experience or situation. Focus on surviving and thriving.

10. Use your own creativity and ingenuity to move through this experience with grace. Think outside the box. How would your favorite hero or heroine behave in this situation?

"When you were born, you cried and the world rejoiced. Live your life so that when you die, the world cries and you rejoice."

Indian Proverb

PART 4

BACKROADS, ALTERNATE
ROUTES & TRAILBLAZING

"Courage is not the absence of fear,
but rather the judgment that something else
is more important than fear."

Ambrose Redmoon

Chapter 16

THE GOOD NEWS GARAGE

"Power concedes nothing without a demand.
It never did and it never will."

– Frederick Douglass

By Hal Colston & Nancy Irwin

SUPPOSE I LEARNED to be an idealist and a trailblazer from my father. My dad was the first African-American in York, Pennsylvania, to be an independent insurance agent. Instead of copying others' success, he set out to create his own. Perhaps that trained me to see what is not and what should be, find others who agree, and co-create it.

My background is in electrical engineering and geology. Somehow in the midst of my college studies, I got sucked in to the restaurant business, becoming a chef, restaurant manager and eventually instructor and catering director at the New England Culinary Institute's Inn at Essex in Vermont. Coming from Philadelphia to Vermont in 1989 with my wife and three children was like going to a foreign country. Our friends were stunned and I was asked over and over, "why are you doing this?" I remembered saying that I didn't know why I felt this need to go there, but I believed we would find out when we got there.

Around age 40, I hit what people typically call a "midlife crisis." I just realized I needed a change. I was ready to take another risk of my own. In spite of my great job as the opening chef at the Capitol Plaza Hotel in Montpelier, Vermont, I was burning out working 80 hours a week there. So I quit and went to work for a non-profit in Burlington, Vermont, called Community Action Agency, which provided direct services to people in poverty. The simple, feel-good fulfillment I got from it was so refreshing after the rat race and endless stress of life I'd left. At Community Action I was able to reconnect to my roots of social justice, having grown up in a racially divided town during the 1960s. Somehow I was able to continue to support my wife and three kids working at this non-profit organization, although Beverly thought that making a lot less money was a little crazy. Yet, learning the ropes for the first time in the social service sector fed my passion to make a difference.

I had an epiphany in 1993, which was a few years after I'd made the career transition. I'm pretty handy, and one day I tried to help get the faulty brakes fixed on a used car a woman with two children on welfare had just bought for $500. I was outraged that she was a victim of a predatory used car dealer with a reputation of exploiting low-income people. Although I was not able to find a just resolution for the woman, it just hit me: how about rehabbing donated used cars for low-income people? The idea just popped in my head that we needed a community-based garage helping people where they are, like a community-health agency.

Lutheran Social Services of New England was in the planning stages of developing its first program in Vermont. My pastor, Connie Parvey, invited me to join the 15-member group composed of representatives from five different area Lutheran congregations. They focused on "who is our neighbor" and "what are the needs of our neighbors," and tried to understand what type of programming would help. I was asked to join their key informant survey. The results of that survey showed a clear problem of transportation equity—there was a huge need among low-income people who struggled because they had no access to any kind of reliable transportation. It was determined that our public transit system was not viable to serve the needs of many low-income people who worked second-shift jobs. The committee had no idea what to do, and there was no program in place. I had a one-page proposal about my garage idea, but at first I didn't have the nerve to present it, because I thought they would think the idea was crazy. It was like a Pentecostal moment. When the group heard the idea, all of them were overwhelmed with excitement.

That was the start of "The Good News Garage."

Setting up office in a local Lutheran church, I started writing grants in my free time while working with a mechanic out of a donated space at the municipal bus garage. I also worked part-time at a bakery to support my family. There were a few tough years in there, but I just knew it would work out. I always feel that answers are right in front of me. So I just kept going forward. Things really took off after about three years.

The Good News Garage has now expanded to Connecticut, New Hampshire and Massachusetts. We've provided reliable, affordable cars to more than 3,000 people, helping them to work, transport their children to school and activities, and to get off welfare in over 50% of our cases. Our program has really dispelled the myths. Low-income people are maligned, but they don't want to be poor. The *to* in *welfare to work* is really all about transportation. If people can't get there, it's not going to happen. I think it's the last hurdle that we're just starting to deal with—the whole mobility issue.

Fortunately, donations keep pouring in. We have been very blessed. More than 100 communities around the nation have contacted me to help them develop their own programs. We have a partnership with the Americorps Vista program, and I'd like to see a real connection with the federal government. We've gotten some great HUD support and recognition. In the meantime, we have a waiting list of applicants to donate. I think that's what people relate to: knowing that their car is going to transform someone's life. It's an incredible feeling to have this win-win situation for everyone—the donors and the recipients.

I've been blessed to have a wonderful staff and support system to help the organization grow. In 2003 I was accepted into Vermont Leadership Institute, an intensive 10-month training experience to assess and grow your leadership skills. On October 18, I had another epiphany at 7 a.m. in the shower—I decided to quit my job as founding director of the Good News Garage. A month later, after spending two sessions with a personal coach, I had a new vision—NeighborKeepers, breaking the bonds of poverty one family at a time. NeighborKeepers is now a non-profit anti-poverty organization in Burlington, Vermont, that has adopted the "Circles of Support" model, which practices radical hospitality. The mission is to establish healthy relationships between the community and families who wish to increase their resources. It's another win-win situation. Everyone benefits from the power of interdependence as the fabric of community is enhanced through meaningful relationships based on trust and reciprocity. Everyone has access to resources to realize their sense of purpose, to fulfill their dreams and contribute to the common good. Community members and allies work together to eliminate barriers to success in a supportive environment, fostering a more cohesive community, and replacing isolation and dependence.

It's an extraordinary thing to be able to serve others instead of just having a job. I believe we are all given opportunities to help others, and those opportunities are called days. We get them one at a time with no guarantee of tomorrow. One of the most important lessons I continue to learn as a change maker is that I must not worry about that which I cannot control. In many ways this is a faith journey. Just trust and believe that the abilities are within you, and the right answers in front of you.

Chapter 17

DREAM WEAVER

*"Success is creating something original and lasting—whether
it is a company, a work of art, an idea or analysis that influence
others, or a happy and productive family."*

– Linda Chavez

By Sigrid Olsen & Nancy Irwin

I'M A BIG BELIEVER in following your intuition, releasing your fears and
trusting your instincts ... that if you embrace your intuition, it will
guide you to where you belong. It's that inner voice that has always
propelled me toward many different and eclectic ventures: I've worked
for a chiropractor, as an assistant teacher at a Montessori school, and as
an instructor of vegetarian cooking classes.

But something was missing. I was always looking for that next big spark that would ignite a new experience or challenge. Being a can-do self-starter, setting and meeting new challenges has always been my catalyst for change.

So I decided to start a small business making and selling hand-printed clothing and items for the home—I made and sold everything out of my house and I loved it! I loved organizing, the people I was meeting and certainly the creativity of it all—creating original designs, inventing colors and weaving fabrics—it all satisfied my creative hunger.

To take the plunge and make this a business—not just a job or a hobby —was daunting initially. There I was, a single mom with two young children to raise, and I was starting a business! But I continued to listen to my inner voice and plunged ahead and founded Sigrid Olsen in 1984.

Juggling the demands of my growing business with dance lessons, Little League games and day care made me realize that running a company is like running a home. When the kids and the company were in their infancies, they all needed nurturing, coddling and close supervision. Soon, the babies were learning to walk, just as the company began to get on its feet. As adolescents, my teenagers and the company grew at a breathless, dynamic pace. Then, when the kids went off to college and gained their independence, I sold Sigrid Olsen to the clothing giant Liz Claiborne in 1999. Now my children and my company are all grown up and doing well— we even have two grandchildren now. Sigrid Olsen has continued to expand, with 54 retail stores nationwide.

While I remained steadfast with my business, I was always fearful about losing touch with my family and friends; in fact, I'm sure that I let my personal life take a back seat from time to time and missed some important family moments. But now, 23 years later, I feel that aspect of my life is more in balance than ever.

Fortunately, supportive and loving people have always surrounded me. My father and late mother always encouraged me to develop my artistic talents; and my husband and children, as well as my close friends, always keep me grounded. At work, I have a large network of designers, merchandisers, and sales and marketing people who are not just employees and co-workers but friends I admire and respect. I have always considered them my second family. That's why I never quit the business, no matter how tough and formidable it became—you don't quit your family. I felt, and still feel, responsible for everyone who works for me.

But no matter how hard, frustrating, demanding or rewarding, I still relish each day and wake up every morning eager to get going. That inner voice continues to tell me that I am on the correct path and no matter how hard it was in the past, I will always find a way to provide myself with the continuous creative challenge I crave, as well as the opportunity for a satisfying livelihood.

So trust your instincts and be prepared to take each step, each day, one at a time, and don't expect to rise to the top immediately. If you embody your passion and follow your intuition, your rewards will find you.

Chapter 18

HEALING ENERGIES

"All we are is vibration."

– Kenneth Klee, Esq.

By Kenneth Klee, Esq. & Nancy Irwin

MY FORMER LAW FIRM had a policy of sabbaticals for lawyers; for every six years of service, we received three months off. In 1983, I took a sabbatical and traveled to Europe with my wife. As we drove through France, Italy and Western Europe, I reflected on my life: "I'm really blessed. I work for a great law firm, I love practicing law and I have a wonderful wife and two great kids." My only complaint was the constant pain in my upper back and neck I'd had since I attended Harvard Law School. I promised myself that once we got back to the States, I would address it.

I'm a really conservative guy, so it was a bold step for me when I started getting massages. The massages provided temporary relief, but the pain would come back. A few years later, I took the big plunge and went to a chiropractor. Again, the relief lasted for a short time, and the pain returned. And then I actually tried acupuncture. It didn't permanently alleviate the pain either, but it did get rid of some allergies.

Then in 1997, at a retreat at the San Ysidro Ranch, I signed up for something called Reiki massage, which is a Japanese form of alternative healing. Now, I'm what you'd call a healthy skeptic. I want to see things work and understand how they work; I want to know the theory behind a function or claim and be able to test it. But I'm also not afraid to try things, so I thought I would give it a shot. What I got was not a massage but a hands-on session of The Radiance Technique, Authentic Reiki®. The woman never touched me physically. She put her hands around my head and on the front side of my body, and then the back of my body. And at the end of the "massage," I felt like I was floating. I asked her what she did and she said, "I patterned cosmic symbols to activate whole light universal energy in each of your atoms and as the goodness expanded, the darkness dissipated, and that's why you're feeling better."

Whatever it was, it worked.

Since I was feeling so much better, I asked her, "How can I learn how to do this?" "Well, there's this teacher in Los Angeles I can send you to," she answered. So, at age 48, I went to LA in December 1997 and learned how to do The Radiance Technique®— and discovered that Reiki energy has several basic effects. It brings about deep relaxation, destroys energy blockages, detoxifies the system, provides new vitality in the form of healing, provides universal life energy and increases the vibrational frequency of the body. I took the first, second and third degrees of The Radiance Technique from a local teacher; I took the teacher training from an instructor who flew in from Florida; and I took the fourth and fifth degrees from Dr. Barbara Ray, who holds the intact keys of The Radiance Technique. And it was the very first energetic healing modality I ever learned.

Ok, I can hear you saying under your breath, "Huh?" Believe me, I was skeptical, too. I mean, I started off life as an agnostic, but developed belief in God as a young man, not by any great awe-inspiring experience but by looking at the order of the universe and thinking this couldn't be random happenstance, there has to be an organizing principle. Eastern medicine, past lives and karma and all that stuff was just a lot of crap to me, and I didn't buy into it at all. I grew up thinking chiropractors were quacks.

And like I said, I'm a conservative skeptic. If you looked at my resume, it would look something like this:

Graduated from Harvard Law School in 1974

Practiced as a lawyer for Congress in Washington, D.C., for three years

Became a member of the California bar in 1975

Went into private corporate bankruptcy law practice in 1977

Started teaching bankruptcy law an as adjunct at UCLA in 1979

Became a full-time professor at UCLA Law School in 1997

Started my own law firm in 1999 handling large Chapter 11 cases

So I'm your regular guy in a suit. I can see how some people don't understand it—if your frame of reference is your five senses and Western medicine and you only believe there's a physical body and that when you die, that's it … to come to grips with things like energy bodies, souls and more than one life really challenges people at very deep levels. And it's understandable that a great percentage of those people would be resistant as opposed to being open-minded and intrigued the way I was.

It's important to honor people's judgments and self-will and not to be judgmental about what people do. I've come across people who have had anger but didn't want to release it because they viewed it as a motivator and didn't want to let it go.

There are billions of people living in Asia who have used these methods of healing for thousands of years, and if they seem to be doing all right, it's rather arrogant of us Westerners to think that our way is the only way.

I'm so left-brained, so analytical—and it's not quackery or witchcraft, it's very real. And as I began to experience more and more of this and saw the healing properties of all these healing modalities and had physical experiences with these energies, it changed my whole worldview.

After my "Reiki massage" experience, I was determined to know more. Starting in December 1997 and over the course of 14 months, I learned the first and second degrees of The Radiance Technique. Then, in January 1999, I was attracted to pranic healing after a visiting professor from Australia demonstrated it to me. This treatment clears and balances the body/mind/spirit's energy connection. In various cultures, this energy is referred to as *ki, chi* or *prana* and represents the life force that exists in all things.

Of course, I wanted to learn more about that, too, so I attended classes taught by the American Institute of Asian Studies in Southern California. I became a voracious student of pranic healing, and after successfully completing eight to 10 courses and working on numerous case studies became a certified pranic healer. Now I'm trained in and use about 10 other healing techniques as well: Pulsor Healing, Beyonder, Neuro Emotional Technique, Crystal Layouts, Tree of Life Healing, DNA/Theta Healing, the Sedona Method, Norri Healing, Xiang Gong, Invocative Healing, and by the time this book is published, I'm sure there'll be more!

Five years ago, it became clear to me that this was something that was becoming not just a hobby but a *serious* hobby. I formed a 501(c)(3) California non-profit public benefit religious corporation called the Klee Ministry, where I conduct healing sessions and also teach classes such as feng shui, Pulsors, The Radiance Technique and Theta healing. I think my calling is to do some occasional teaching but mostly healing.

I sat next to a reporter from the *Los Angeles Times* one day at a seminar and I told her what I did and invited her over for a healing. She was so impressed, she wrote an article about energy healing, and as a result of that article I got more than 200 calls to perform healings on people.

But this is not my business; it's a hobby. I don't charge for my healing services, but I do accept donations to Klee Ministry. I do all of the Klee Ministry work by donation. People usually donate by cash or check, some a little and some a lot. For those who ask, the "recommended" donation is $200 for a two-hour session. So far, I have not taken anything out of the Ministry in the form of compensation. I use the donations to pay for healing classes and materials and to buy healing items like pulsors, crystals, candles, etc. That may change down the line if the energetic healing work becomes a full time profession. And if they can't donate, I suggest to them to say a prayer or at least have some energetic exchange. But if they do make a donation, I bless it to increase the good karma that resides in them. I don't give out supplements or herbs because I'm not a licensed herbologist. I let my clients know that I'm not a physician or licensed by the state as a doctor, I'm not going to diagnose their illness and I don't discourage anyone from seeing a physician. By law, energy healers in California have to have their clients sign a consent form stating as much.

Several years ago, I became a minister of the Universal Life Church so I could officiate at weddings. I am not recognized in all states, but being a minister helps support my healing ministry. I also became admitted to the Rabbinic program at the Academy for Jewish Religion, with plans to take classes including Hebrew. I wanted to learn Hebrew so I could study Kabbalah and actually read the original Aramaic and Hebrew commentary and have my own interpretation of it, because the Kabbalistic work that I've done is extremely powerful.

I found—and still find—it fascinating that a whole world can exist that is different than the world most people know. I keep telling my wife, "We don't have to watch The X-Files, we live it." I think science is going to establish the credibility of all this some day. The apparatus that can measure this energy just hasn't been invented yet, but when it is, it's going to turn the world upside down.

Other energy healers have asked me to work in their centers and share space, but—and here's where the left part of my brain takes over—I'm writing a book on bankruptcy and the Supreme Court. Naturally, I am calling it *Bankruptcy and the Supreme Court,* and it will be published by Matthew Bender & Co., probably in 2009. I'm not going anywhere until that book's written.

I find that working as a healer increases my energy. I do a limited amount of self-healing, go to a very gifted acupuncturist, see a massage therapist once a month and have sessions with a wonderful energy healer chiropractor four times a year. Occasionally I do self-healing, but not obsessively, I'm more involved with healing others than myself. Many times when I'm healing someone, I feel myself being healed.

As for obstacles, I've encountered a few problems between my law practice and my teaching where I wanted to take various courses and wasn't able. But I think things work out in God's time, not necessarily my time, and when I'm ready for things they seem to happen. (Even when I'm not ready for them they seem to happen!)

Some of my partners think I'm crazy, and who knows what this will do to my expert witness work. But I'll tell you, as a result of the *LA Times* article, I got contacted by a group of lawyers who wanted me for one of their cases. They had a client who was an acupuncturist on trial and they asked me to be an expert witness about the nature of the acupuncture business and the energy movement.

My advice for people stuck on the crossroads of life is that we all have procedures that allow us to make choices—even if it's from the analytical side, writing a list of pluses and minuses and then prioritizing it. Or you can go inside yourself and look at your life now and consider your options. Alternate between feeling what it would be like to do one thing and what it would be like not to do it; you'll get a good indication from your subconscious and super-conscious about the direction in which you should move. Just imagine what it would feel like to leave your profession and do something else—really feel it.

I was one of the last guys, I thought, who'd ever get involved in this realm.

If anyone had told me 20 to 25 years ago that I'd be working as an energy healer, I would have laughed in his face. Just think of me as a UCLA law professor and prominent corporate bankruptcy lawyer who happens to practice energy healing on the side.

Chapter 19

FINDING THE WAY OUT

"It is more important to live the life one wishes to live
and to go down with it if necessary, quite contentedly, than
to live more profitably but less happily."
– Marjorie Kinnan Rawlings

By Anonymous & Nancy Irwin

A FTER HER MASTECTOMY TO remove breast cancer, my mother lay in her hospital bed, looked up at me and said, "At least I can say I have lived a great and full life." It was at that moment I realized that I was still waiting for my full life to begin. I'd always been a housewife, and only worked every once in a while as a landscape architect. As I got married about two weeks after graduation, my degree in landscape architecture started gathering dust. My husband entered the Navy, and we moved around for most of the first three years of our married life. I worked where and when I could in landscaping, but sad to say, my husband treated this as my little side-line that was only acceptable as long as it didn't interfere with his schedule, meals, etc.—and somehow, I bought into that thinking. Then I had little children, and tried to keep up limited design work on the side.

For years, my husband had told me in subtle and not-too-subtle ways that I would always be dependent on him and would never be able to break free and take care of myself. He kept most of our finances hidden from me. Looking back, I'm amazed I put up with this, but my generation was programmed to believe that women should marry, have children and take care of their families; divorce was not an option.

I kept feeling my life was out of balance, like vertigo. I was doing my best and waiting for things to get better. I tried to expand my professional career, but the lack of support at home made it impossible. At last, I got fed up with being treated like I was beholden to my husband and wasting my opportunities to accomplish something significant. I decided to take charge of my life. What I needed was a regular, decent income that could support my daughters and myself.

I started by doing small jobs from home and volunteering. I soon realized I had a lot more practical sense than most of the other volunteers with whom I was working, and I discovered I was not a "spendthrift" or "absent-minded," as my husband had convinced me. Thanks to my accomplishments with the organization, I was eventually elected local chapter president. I then served on national committees, ultimately becoming the president of the entire national organization.

At first, my husband had thought the volunteer work was suitable "for a housewife." But soon he started complaining about my involvement and tried to make me feel bad by insinuating it was unimportant and a waste of time. He even tried to bully me by acting unreasonably strict on our children. Things were pleasant at home only when everyone in the house catered to him—otherwise, we were all subjected to his raging temper.

Getting out of that environment, even for a few hours here and there, was my first step to changing. Being appreciated for my efforts was very rewarding. In fact, the positive feedback from others made me realize that I was settling for a home situation I could change. But actually making that change, mentally and physically, took years. It would be 14 years, in fact, after my first venture as a volunteer that I finally left my husband. It took another three or four years after that to really get on my feet. Part of the delay was my fear of taking our young daughters out into the real world and not being able to take care of them.

Another fear that haunted me was the fear of failure. As a lawyer, my husband made sure I would get nothing when we divorced. Lawyers know many ways to hide assets. Our younger daughter, 15 at the time, was with me, and her father would give her a few hundred dollars here and there, but managed to "legally" report a low income to reduce his child support obligation. This was all part of his scheme to pressure me into folding and running back home a failure.

My parents were my primary support system through the ordeal and backed me up so much that I had to calm *them* down when my ex got out of hand. My younger daughter and I moved in with them for a number of years, but both daughters told me I was doing the right thing.

I endured many unexpected obstacles. There was of course my lack of money, and then my lack of job experience because I'd been out of the working world for so long. I also had to overcome the "programmed to fail" mentality that had been drummed into me for years. And to top it off, I was a single mom trying to raise a rebellious teenager. Two months after we moved in with my parents, my dad, who had been struggling with heart and lung problems, got worse and was placed in intensive care. He died three months later. At about the same time, my mother's breast cancer returned and she underwent chemotherapy. My daughter's actions went from being a big help to a terror. All this was happening while I was trying to start a career with a design/construction company.

Some friends stuck by me during this time, some acted like I had lost my mind and some actually started treating me like a "threat"—as if I might be competition for their husbands. Women who leave their husbands face a social barrier, especially in a small, conservative Deep-South town like mine. Some of my male colleagues were great and supportive, and others looked at me as a new divorcee and "fair game." But overall my business associates were very encouraging, as were my parents and daughters.

My primary focus was that I was not going to return to my previous life—no matter what. I was not going to fail! The thought of it made me feel like I couldn't breathe. I've never regretted the decision I made and would do it all over again if I had to. When I found myself mired in that "fearful" stage we all go through when we're trying something new, I always asked myself, "Why not?" and "If not now, when?" One thing about fear is that it is a self-defeating habit. Start breaking that habit, and the freedom will translate into all areas of your life.

My advice, if you're considering making a transition in midlife, is to ask yourself, "Is there a reason?" To women who have not worked outside the home and are not financially independent, I would say that independence can be a tough road, so be sure it's not something you're considering just on a whim. Also, be mindful that you'll have to make many sacrifices and changes—but it is well worth the effort.

Be sure to look for role models if you don't have them in your life. My mother has always been mine. She was constantly strong and optimistic, even in the roughest of times—including when my dad was dying and she was suffering with cancer. Even now, when things in my life go bad, I always try to live up to this standard.

If possible, make some financial plans to see you through. Go back to school for a new degree, perhaps, or take any job to get your foot back into the workforce. You'll find you can do all sorts of things you never tried and, believe me, accomplishments are empowering.

Today, I'm a successful landscape-architectural business owner. I enjoy close relationships with my two daughters, who, I'm proud to say, are independent young ladies. During the Christmas season a couple of years after I "broke out," a friend asked me if I honestly did not have a moment of regret, especially during the holidays. My answer was an exuberant: "Not even for a microsecond!"

Chapter 20

FROM CRITIC TO MEDIC

"The journey of a thousand miles starts with a single step."
– Ancient Chinese Saying

By Thomas Boeker, M.D., Ph.D.

MY MIDLIFE AWAKENING INVOLVED a transition from art to science, from unquestioned assumption to untested hypothesis. I started my journey with a Ph.D. in theatre, and I spent more time working as a theatre critic than as a professor—though neither occupation paid very well. In fact, only two theatre critics in Chicago made a living wage, writing for the *Sun Times* and the *Tribune*, and I wasn't one of them. So I had a day job teaching seminars in the interpretation of literature and reviewing plays in the evenings and on weekends. I was never very artistic or academic, despite the Ph.D., but I was a fair writer and a much better critical thinker. It was a fun job, and I always got good seats.

But the time came when I wanted to make a change because I felt I wasn't going anywhere—living day to day like college students half my age made my life seem marginal and frivolous. Then one day, while reading *Man's Fate* by Andre Malraux, a line stuck in my head: "the theatre is not serious; the bullfight is serious." As a critic, I was just a sideliner, a master of the obvious. What I needed was some sort of existential redemption, but I was in doubt as to my ability to forge a new way of life.

I had many negative and limiting beliefs to overcome. Like most people who hit the wall of middle age, I had much more belief in my potential and myself as a younger man, but now it seemed as if that was just the narcissism and untested bravado of youth. After that wore off, I was left with a poor opinion of myself.

So I decided to take it one step at a time. Finally, I made a very important decision. When I told my dad I wanted to go to medical school, I asked him not to discuss it with the rest of the family; I was unsure of my resolve. It would be a long journey to an unknown place, I knew. I'm still on that journey. I try to keep my eyes open every step of the way, but I still stumble. Mostly I stumble over facts and they change the way I see the world—which is how it should be. I plan to keep stumbling ahead until I drop dead!

On the flip side of that decision was fear, and I became my biggest obstacle. I was afraid that, at age 40, I was too old to go to medical school. I was afraid I wasn't smart enough. I was afraid of death, afraid of failure. I was afraid that my ability to memorize (a fundamental skill essential to doctors as well as actors) had diminished. I was afraid I lacked the ability to make such a substantial change in my life. I was afraid that my decision to go into medicine, that my very curiosity, might take me into a dark and hostile world. Most of all, I was afraid of stagnation.

But my overwhelming sense of curiosity, stubbornness and even my debts kept me going, and I plowed through my fear, attended medical school and now am a psychiatrist in private practice.

Age discrimination is real and it was another obstacle I had to overcome. I think medical school and residency training can be so stressful that some unconscious factors come into play. It was not unusual for a supervising physician to be a dozen or more years younger than I was. In terms of object relations psychology, I played (in the supervising physician's mind) the role of a father figure, but the power structure was reversed. Medical students are at the very bottom of the food chain in the world of medicine, outranked even by nurses. This became very apparent to me during my surgery rotation, when sleep-deprived resident physicians, some of whom may have been pressured by their parents into med school, acted out their hostile and punitive fantasies upon me. I was abused and infantilized. At first it made me angry. But a friend visited me on the surgical service one day. He waved his hand around the surgical ICU, referring to all the ill-tempered doctors surrounding us as "passing shadows." He was right. So are we all.

Luckily, my support systems were firmly in place. My father was and continues to be very supportive. My girlfriend, Lucy, started medical school even later in life than I; she's been very supportive and has been the greatest inspiration in my life. Some friends in med school and friends from my former life were also supportive.

Knowing what I know now, I'm pretty sure I would do things differently. I discovered that I had a lot more reserve capacity in my character than I had believed. Sometimes I sell myself short. Things seem out of reach sometimes, but we really don't know that for sure unless we reach for them; maybe if we stretch, we can increase our reach. Kids do this all the time. It's how we grow. After everything I've been through would I have gone to medical school? Who knows? Actually, I've been thinking lately about tackling yet another field, but I don't want to accrue any more student debt.

Any career transition requires retooling, either through education or apprenticeship. There are financial risks, of course, which you have to judge for yourself. So much depends on what goal or goals you have set. It's not realistic, for instance, to become a major league baseball player or prima ballerina at age 40. So, define your goal. Decide what you're willing to sacrifice to attain that goal. Research the field that you want to go into. Do you think you can survive in that line of work? Can you grow and build a career in that area? What assets, backgrounds and proclivities do you have to bring to that field, especially ones that would distinguish you and make you more successful than the young bucks in that same job?

And, if like me, you've hit the fearful stage, just remember that a lot of fear is simply caused by the unknown. It helps to examine the nature of the thing that you fear. This can be done by education or confrontation, what I like to call "naming the beast." This way, familiarity can separate out the things that are reasonably feared from the things that are fearful products of our ignorance, imagination or childhood misperceptions, from the things that are reasonably feared, like grizzly bears. I suggest standing tall and, at the same time, backing slowly away. Then, on your next trip through the woods, take the long way around.

Chapter 21

LEARN TO BELIEVE

---

*"Isn't it nice to think that tomorrow is a new day
with no mistakes in it yet!"*

– Anne of Green Gables

By Mariaemma Pelullo-Willis & Nancy Irwin

E VERYONE IS BORN WITH something they are supposed to be doing. You just have to discover for yourself what that "something" is. Don't let anybody else scare you from doing what you feel is right for you—just go for it!

As a veteran educator, I have dedicated my life to finding ways to help every child become a learning success story. After earning a bachelor's degree in psychology, a master's in education, and California

Life Teaching Credentials for regular and special education, I became the director of a private center for children with learning disabilities. But after working with these great kids for 11 years, I realized that it's not the kids who have a disability, but the system in which they are taught. Kids are like square pegs, and if they don't fit in to the round hole of current education standards, dysfunctional labels such as ADD, dyslexic, hyperactive or learning disabled are applied. School labels are ingrained in us forever—all of those negative messages are detrimental to a child's growth, and soon a child internalizes, "I'm not smart enough" or "I can't do that" and might refuse to see his/her potential.

We need to teach everyone to be positive and to give kids the tools they need to do what they want with their lives. People come with their own toolbox containing everything they need to succeed. We just have to help them discover for themselves the skills and talents they already possess. The truth is, we all learn in different ways and fall into one or more of these learning styles: tactile/kinesthetic, or learning from touch and movement; visual-picture, which is learning by what you see; visual-print, which is learning from the written page; auditory-listening, which is learning by hearing; and auditory-verbal, which is learning by talking.

Between 50% and 60% of the population are tactile/kinesthetic learners; about 20% are visual-picture learners; and about 15% are listening/verbal learners. The rest (only about 5%) are print learners. Yet our classrooms are set up mainly for print learners: "Read the chapter and answer the questions. Read a book and write a book report. Read the textbook and study for the test. Read out loud to the class. Fill out workbooks and worksheets. Take written notes." That's why only three to five kids in every classroom get all the A's! It's not that these few are really more intelligent ... the other 90% to 95% are simply not print learners and these print strategies do not work for them.

Frustrated, I knew there was a better way to teach, and I started searching for my own methods. My quest included interviewing professionals in the field, researching alternative education methods and participating in a variety of workshops. I discovered the whole field of learning styles, which had never been taught in teacher training. The results left me excited and eager to try something different, and I was passionate about sharing this knowledge. At last, I made the big move: I left my director position and went into private practice as a tutor. This turn allowed me to explore, invent and practice teaching to different styles, using various methods. The results were magical—the ideas I developed and implemented began making a difference in the way these children were processing information and learning.

I continued to tutor and began offering workshops, and in 1988 I met Victoria Kindle Hodson, a kindred spirit who attended my "Educating for Self Esteem" workshop. We immediately hit it off. We both knew there was something wrong with the education system, and we both wanted to change it. A week later, we were developing strategies and our education model, "LearningSuccess™." We then created our own learning style assessments and began presenting our material at conferences and working with home school-based communities. Over the next 10 years, Victoria and I experienced such positive feedback and results that we started to think bigger.

We always thought that what we were advocating would make a great book but had never acted on it. Then, one day in 1998, there was a message on my machine: "This is Prima Publishing, and we would like to be your publisher." The company had seen an article I had written for a home-school newspaper and a couple of books I had previously self-published on education topics.

Victoria and I both had guaranteed income from tutoring and conducting workshops, so taking time away for creating a whole book was a scary step, but we knew we had to do it. How else could parents find out the truth about how children learn, and how to coach their children for learning success, even if schools were not doing so? Published in 1999, *Discover Your Child's Learning Style* was written as a how-to guide for parents and teachers, helping adults and children discover their unique learning needs. The publisher had originally wanted us to do a book for the homeschooling population, and we were thrilled when they suggested the more inclusive title, since it would benefit anyone raising and teaching children.

After the book was published, the whole theme of "learning success" really took off and kept evolving. We founded The LearningSuccess Institute, developed a LearningSuccess Coach Certification Training Program, and now we have certified coaches conducting training and doing learning style consultations for children, families, and adults on the job. I have also co-authored *Midlife Crisis Begins in Kindergarten*, written *RealLife™ Electives: Life Success Formula and Money Formula*, and written a chapter for the book *Inspiration to Realization: Learn to Receive as Much as You Give*.

My vision was 20 years in the making, but I knew this was what I was supposed to be doing with my life. While Victoria and I both were well into our 40s when we veered off onto our own path, I always felt so strongly that people just had to know there were better educational means for children, and that kept me going. It also helped to have a great support system—my husband. From my very first conference, he encouraged me, helped lug all the materials to meeting rooms and set up booths. There was no money from my business at that point—we paid for our booths ourselves and got the cheapest motel rooms possible—but it was well worth it in the end.

My advice? Listen and learn. Find mentors to help give you the confidence you lack and to cheer you on. Make the most of books, audiotapes and motivational speakers to keep you on a positive track—I spent so many years wondering if I was doing the right thing and doubting my abilities. Also, if you don't know how to do something, find someone who can (for me, it was getting people who know how to market, advertise, etc.). Trial and error take time, and I lost years to the learning curve by doing everything myself.

When I look back at everything, I can't believe I've accomplished so much, becoming both a speaker and an author. And I've never stopped dreaming. That's the thing about goals—they're always evolving. My dream now is to have certified LearningSuccess Coaches all over the world, and to have the freedom to write and do more public appearances, perhaps even TV.

In the education field, my work is considered very controversial. My peers say I'm not following the rules. But I never let it bother me—I took on my critics. So don't be afraid. Don't listen to the negativity that surrounds you. Listen to the positive people who can help guide you down the path to your success and fulfillment—and just go for it!

Chapter 22

SYNCHRONICITY

"When tillage begins, other arts follow.
The farmers, therefore, are the founders of human civilization."
– Daniel Webster

By Emanuel Culman & Nancy Irwin

FROM 1981 TO 1988, I was the director of a small, contemporary art gallery in downtown Los Angeles. Representing only a handful of artists, my wife and I struggled to keep the gallery's doors open. And we found ourselves struggling, too. We went through a divorce, and an agonizing international child-custody battle ensued. As a result of the ongoing turmoil, I suffered a bout with depression.

At this time, I was in my late 40s and looking for something that would lift me up and give me a sense of purpose once again. I was introduced to Kundalini Yoga—a meditative discipline that consists of a set of simple techniques of breath, movement, stretching, meditation and relaxation to create a communication between mind and body. Kundalini Yoga stimulated my mind's potential and reawakened my desire to heal myself and move on with my life.

A new love, Cheryl, entered my life and helped prop me up in so many ways. I soon developed a successful home-restoration business in Beverly Hills. But then came another devastating crash—the chemicals I had been ingesting all those years restoring homes made me seriously ill. Unable to pull through easily, I found myself closing the doors on yet another business.

Utilizing the Kundalini Yoga techniques I had learned, I meditated on the fragmented energy within me and consciously sent out messages that would attract the people I needed to help heal me. The synchronicity that followed was astonishing. The right people and events came into my life just when I needed them and my inner and outer roadblocks gave way to a whole new dimension of living and learning.

I decided to share the restorative talents of the healers who helped me, and I thought, what better medium than TV? A program on Public Access was just the beginning. This venture grew and grew, and my wife, Cheryl Planert, and I co-produced and I hosted more than 150 programs, broadcasting up to 40 shows per month across as many as 16 channels in the Los Angeles area. This show *Changes* brought me lots of exposure and a chance to meet brilliant people. Applying what I learned from my guests, I went back to a novel, *The Prodigal Daughter of Taquinta*, I had written nine years prior and fleshed it out into a screenplay. Its fifth rewrite is almost complete and I am currently looking for funding.

At age 59, I made another you-turn. My wife and I were really ready to leave Los Angeles and took our time "shopping" for a place to live. Using astrocartography, an astrologer told me that for artistic expression and success, I should relocate to around the 48th parallel— which runs through North Dakota, of all places! On our way to meet with a local realtor in Dickinson, North Dakota, we saw that an old movie theatre was for sale. All the pieces fell into place very quickly and serendipitously. We bought the Bijou Theatre, a charming old 1940s vintage theatre in Beach, North Dakota, which is reminiscent of the hill country around my hometown, Leeds, England (but much drier!). I'm still stunned that I actually own a theatre!

The now-named Bijou Show House presents not only newly released films, but also live performances on the stage I built. We stage events with local university students, readings by authors and performances by musicians and entertainers. We screen empowering films (including a 2008 Academy Award contender) to encourage adults and children to see the commonalities and to celebrate the differences of the human race. In this exquisite rural community, this theatre is a metaphor for life: it's pure potential.

Chapter 23

YOU CAN FLY

"Believe and ye shall achieve."

– Anonymous

By Connie Zack & Nancy Irwin

B EFORE GETTING IN TOUCH with my entrepreneurial spirit, I spent 11 years climbing the corporate ladder at Procter & Gamble. I had numerous positions in pharmaceutical sales, marketing and category management. My last position there was as the category manager for the Gastrointestinal Division of Procter and Gamble Pharmaceuticals. I was responsible for providing the direction and deploying the marketing materials and tools to the GI organization. I eventually made my way into the company's staff being groomed for future executive positions.

I loved my work, but at the end of the day I was still working for someone else. Yearning to use my leadership expertise in my own way and on my own terms, I started looking for that opportunity that all restless entrepreneurs seek. It was very hard to let go of my job security, but seizing an active role as a key decision-maker was thrilling because I was able to focus my leadership ability in an area of my own passion and will. And once I took that leap, I learned I could fly!

In 2002, after taking out loans on all my assets—home, stocks, everything—I found the strength to break out and invest all my money and time in my own company, Sunlight Saunas. Now I know what you're thinking—from pharmaceuticals to saunas? But both are health-related industries. Instead of using traditional convection heat, Sunlight Saunas use far-infrared light, the safest and most healing of the sun's rays. Emanating a deep, penetrating heat, the far-infrared waves raise a person's body core temperature. Some of the therapeutic benefits include weight loss, lower blood pressure, increased circulation and pain relief for sufferers of fibromyalgia (chronic fatigue syndrome), sore joints and more. With great joy, I found tremendous success with my company. As chief sales and marketing officer, I have doubled the company's annual sales each year since its inception. I am proud to be one of the nine women who made it to *Entrepreneur* magazine's "Hot 100" List of 2004. Sunlight Saunas also made the "Hot 100 List" in 2005 and 2006 and won the Inc. 500 award in 2006.

I'm very proud of my accomplishments because I knew my vision had value. I didn't follow the rules—I followed my gut, listened to my own voice and never strayed from my focus.

My advice to anyone thinking about venturing out on their own is to narrow your scope—pick an area of interest and jump in. So many people spread themselves too thin and never become experts at anything. You'll be surprised at how much you can improve any area of your life just by focusing on it. Other helpful tips:

1. Define your picture of success for any given task and then work backward, outlining the logical steps it will take to get there. Keep

a daily log of your progress so that you can stay on track and see how far you've come!

2. Practice the art of negotiation. Too many people think success is black and white. In my experience, hearing a "no" is just the beginning of the process of refining a clearer path to the "yes."

3. Develop active listening skills. People are usually communicating a lot more than just what they say. Pay attention to the tone of voice, eye contact, body language and phrasing. Communication is always more effective when you are responding to the entire message being conveyed.

4. Practice being present. When you are having a conversation, treat that person as though they are the only person on earth. So many successful opportunities are missed when your mind is not totally focused on the task at hand. When you are fully present, you will find that the quality of your relationships, as well as the quality of your life experience, deepens tremendously.

5. Let your motivation be natural and don't compare yourself to others. Avoid keeping a scorecard of what you have done versus someone else. This only breeds negative energy and takes your focus away from the reason you are doing a good deed. Do things in life because you want to, not because you expect something in return.

6. Find a mentor who, in your eyes, is successful and talk with him or her on a regular basis. Mentoring is a ritual that men do very well naturally, and it's time for women to counsel one another in our areas of expertise. Being guided by the successful tips of a veteran is so much easier than trying to figure everything out on your own. You will also thrive from the support you receive.

7. Invest in your own financial security. Be proactive in expanding your knowledge of your finances and learn what you can do to improve them.

8. Face your fears. It's usually our own insecurities that cause the greatest roadblocks to success. Play out the worst-case scenario in your mind and know that in reality, you can sail through it. Once

you realize that it's just the fear of the unknown holding you back or slowing you down, you will be ready to take that leap that will allow you to fly!

Chapter 24

LIVING WITH PASSION

*"In life you can have what you want, or come up
with excuses as to why you don't have what you want."*

– James Collister

By James Collister & Nancy Irwin

A S I APPROACHED 50, I woke up one morning and asked, "Is this all there is?" I was a successful businessman, had money in the bank, had a family, but I was unhappy with the way my life was going.

The other thing was—and I think this is a common feeling among a lot of married men, especially if it's been a long-term marriage—there was a feeling that in the marriage, our priorities were all out of order. If I were to write out a list of what I presumed were my wife's priorities, the kids would be first, the house would be second, followed by the horses, three blanks spaces and then me at the bottom. My wife probably perceived my priorities to be my business, my mother and father, the employees I had working for me, my kids, a couple of blank spaces and her.

Trying to find companionship and love, thinking that my wife was to blame for all my problems, I eventually had an affair. My wife and I went into counseling and tried to put a happy face on our marriage, but we were both pretty miserable. After the kids left for college, we separated and later divorced.

I dated after the divorce, but six months into a new relationship, the woman would invariably ask, "Where's this heading?" "Out the door," was my typical response. I was fearful of relationships, and commitment was something that I was running away from.

In the course of dating, I joined a dating service, which required that I fill out a questionnaire about who I was, what I did, my goals and aspirations, and my likes and dislikes. Next, I had to write what I was looking for in a relationship, the qualities I admired in a woman and why someone would want to date me. All this made me a bit uncomfortable. Opening myself up like that was not easy, but I began to see the root of my discontent.

As I wrote, I began to realize what I wanted—a woman with a sense of humor, a woman who liked to travel, who liked the theatre, who liked to shop at Victoria's Secret, who liked warm water sports, liked to dance and liked to go out to dinner.

With these wants defined, I soon met several nice ladies. We'd go out, but after a month or two any hopes for a relationship just petered out. I wondered why. Then I realized I had a standard against which I compared each woman—and none measured up! That standard was the first girl I ever dated—Linda McKesson. We were in junior high school, and I was almost 14. I'll never forget our first date—October 29, 1953. We dated off and on through high school, went off to college and never saw each other again.

The more I thought about her, the more determined I became to find her and complete my mythological relationship with her so I could go on in life.

On October 6, 1993, I called our old high school and got the names of the high school reunion committee. A couple of phone calls later, I had Linda's number—should I call? What if she didn't remember me? Worse, what if she remembered me and didn't want to talk to me? I heard she was married—what if her husband answered the phone?

I held my breath and dialed the number. She answered, and after a few minutes of reintroduction, it seemed that the 35 years we'd been apart melted away. She sounded just like she did the last time we spoke. When she told me that she was in the process of getting a divorce, my heart excitedly skipped a beat.

We met for lunch the very next day—almost 30 years to the day of our first date— and I boldly told her, "I've been in love with you my entire life and I'll be in love with you forever and we're going to get married."

October 19, 1996, was our wedding day. The first morning of our honeymoon in Sonoma, I looked at my new bride and knew I wanted to spend every moment of every day with her. That's when I decided to get out of my management-consulting firm; six weeks later, I sold the company and essentially retired.

We traveled, and in the process of traveling, I was reading and experiencing love, romance and marriage—what it's like to have a soul mate and to be a man willing to acknowledge I have a soul mate. During my first marriage, I took a variety of personal-awareness seminars and began to understand what was involved in a relationship. And here I was in my second marriage, so blissfully happy and finally applying everything I had learned years before. When Linda and I began dating, we had examined our images of the ideal mate and how they affected our relationships. Together we began to design our relationship principles. It was then I decided to write my book, *The Last Relationship Book You'll Need: Mastering the Five Universal Principles*.

The five principles I've discovered and that I wrote about in my book form the foundation of a successful and loving relationship:

1. Trust
2. Communication
3. Respect
4. Commitment
5. Consciousness.

And the seven points that we can all live by—whether you're in a relationship with someone else or with yourself—are:

1. Live with passion
2. Be grateful
3. Be patient
4. Remember I am the observer and speaker of my life
5. Share my heart
6. Be willing to receive
7. Find a way to serve others.

Now in my second career as author and a lifestyle and relationship coach, I've conducted hundreds of seminars focusing on creating strong personal and business relationships, effective communication and personal growth.

When I do seminars and tell our relationship story, people approach me and declare, "Well, that's great that it happened to you, but that's a once-in-a-lifetime event, that's never going to happen to me." The story we tell is our relationship story created by us as we lived. Will yours be the same? Probably not. But if you're open to committing to the relationship, these principles can allow you to invent, design, and create your own story of companionship and bliss.

Just remember that a successful relationship involves a bringing together of the two halves of what it means to be human, not the masculine and feminine, but the spiritual god and goddess that we already are.

I've learned a lot on this journey: that failure is just a part of success and that in the words of Helen Keller, "Life is either an exciting adventure, or nothing!"

One day in January 2006, my wife gave me a "honey do." This was not unusual, but for some unknown reason before I filled her request, I said: "OK, but first a kiss." This became a ritual we played out two or three times a day. It sounds sappy, but for us, it was a special way for us to create our love. One beautiful morning in May, I was getting dressed to go present a seminar. Linda asked me to take the trash out before I left. She smiled as I said the now-familiar words, "OK, but first a kiss." It was a lovely spring day, and Lionel Richie's song "Endless Love" was playing on the CD player. I swept my beautiful wife into my arms, and the kiss turned into a dance through that whole romantic song. I looked into her eyes and told her "You will always be *my* endless love." Then I took out the trash and went to my meeting.

Little did I know those would be my last words to her. When I returned home at 10:30, I found her lying on the floor. She'd had a massive heart attack and did not survive. She was just shy of her 65th birthday.

I'm still stunned that after only 13 years of bliss with my endless love, it's all over. Love *is* endless; life, unfortunately, is not. Linda loved dolphins, and I started the Linda Collister Memorial Endowment Fund for Dolphins at the University of Hawaii to keep her spirit alive. It may sound crazy, but I always felt that Linda and I were like those frolicking, jolly creatures—leaping joyously, celebrating life.

Our life together was sparkling and beautiful ... and yours can be, too. Just keep kissing and dancing.

As I write this, I relive our time together and tears of joy and pain come to my eyes. My heart swells and breaks as I remember all those wonderful days and that single day of May 18. Linda always loved telling our story and I appreciate your reading it now.

Lest you think this story has an unhappy ending, let me give you a happy addendum. The principles I wrote about and learned to put into action with Linda really do work. I have a new woman in my life. Her name is Barbara and she is the daughter of some longtime friends of my parents. When we met, we discovered we have several important similar interests—travel, food and golf. Our first date was a golf outing, and when she hit her first drive I said to myself "Wow, did she hit that good. Now this could be interesting. She really looks good in that golf outfit too!" We dated and I went through all the shoulds and what-ifs. Should I be dating this soon after losing my soul mate? What will people think? How can I be developing feelings for her?

As I asked all these questions I realized that Barbara and I were developing a truly close friendship, and I recalled that great Nietzsche quote: "It's not the lack of love that kills relationships, it is the lack of friendship." Barbara and I created friendship and companionship. We discussed our interests and goals for our own future lives and began to see that we were in tune with each other and headed in the same direction. The shoulds and what-ifs began to lose importance just in the process of reclaiming my life and moving on. I realized that line from the movie *The Shawshank Redemption* was correct: "Either get on with living or get on with dying," and I chose living. Would Linda approve? I think she would, but she is not here in this life any longer, I am. She will always be the first love and now I realize I can have more than one love. Barbara is now my love and the feelings I create with her are no different than I created with Linda—respect, dignity, honesty, humor. We create our relationships not in the past and not in the future, we create them in each and every moment of NOW, NOW, NOW. When I live in the NOW my true quality of the soul comes forth and the true quality and experience of the soul is happy, joyous and free. If we are willing to live in the NOW, this is how we experience our life.

By the time this book goes to press, Barbara and I will be married and have moved into a new home we are building in La Quinta, California. Of *course* it is on a golf course! We will honeymoon in Canada at a resort area Barbara has been to in the past that is right in the middle of the wine, food and golf area of Canada. Heaven. We both talk about our past mates, but not too much—this is now and that was then. Love is not some THING you fall into. Love, respect and dignity are conditions you create for yourself and invite others to dance with you. Barbara and I dance together and I can truly say I love her. This is not the story of life I ever expected I would live, especially 30 to 40 years ago. Barbara tells me that I am not the guy she expected, and I am living proof that you can not only change, but you can have what you want if you are willing to accept each moment of NOW in life and be grateful.

I believe that all life is just a series of events and stories we invent about them. Life is truly an exciting adventure and I count my blessings. If anyone reads my story they will have to say "Well there goes one lucky SOB!" I agree but I think we make our own luck. Dodgers shortstop Maurie Wills once defined luck as "when preparation meets opportunity." Everyone can prepare themselves for relationship and when the opportunity appears they can really have all they want and more.

Chapter 25

LEARN TO CHANGE

"There is not effort without error and shortcomings."
– Theodore Roosevelt

By Jan Bartlett & Nancy Irwin

I'VE ALWAYS NEEDED NEW challenges to keep me going. One look at my resume and you'll notice that I was a medical technologist for many years before entering TV news and radio broadcasting. Then, after 15 years in show business, the Screen Actors Guild went on strike and I found myself without work. To make ends meet, I began working as an elementary school substitute teacher. I found myself drawn to early education because I wanted the chance to make a real difference in children's lives.

This opportunity to effect change—to step in and help a child start on the path to getting an education and realize his or her dreams—made my years in show business seem frivolous and insignificant. I soon came to the eye-opening realization that substitute teaching to subsidize my movie and TV career wasn't enough. I decided, at age 50, to get my credentials and teach full time.

Substitute teaching all day meant that the only time I could attend school was in the evenings and on weekends. It involved two years and a tremendous amount of work, some of which was helpful and some not so worthwhile. And I have to admit, I gave my instructors a hard time if I found them lacking in knowledge of the subject or their ability to teach it. But I've always considered myself a survivor and never want to admit that any situation can get the best of me. I don't know if I'd call it stupidity or stubbornness, but I don't quit easily. Through it all, my two daughters and son-in-law were, and remain, my unwavering support system.

My transition was fairly smooth. Starting over in my new career, I discovered that most people I worked with were extremely helpful and forgiving of mistakes. Teachers are, by nature, a friendly and nurturing group and will carry you along on their shoulders until you can walk on your own.

After receiving my credentials and starting to teach full time, I unfortunately began comparing myself with my own elementary teachers. Because memories are imperfect, I had idealized them to the point that I felt I could never measure up, and so I feared being inadequate in comparison. I am a perfectionist, and it was impossible to find the time to do everything to perfection ... or even close to perfection. Teaching is like housework ... there is no endpoint, and for someone like me who likes to reach an endpoint, it's frustrating when there isn't one. I still haven't mastered this, and I get unhappy with myself when I can't do it all.

But don't let that happen to you—for God's sake, jump in! There is nothing to be afraid of. Keep your game face on, pay attention, work hard and ask for help when you need it. I have found most people to be good, helpful advocates who love to share their expertise with others. Nothing is worse than a mediocre life, and I refuse to sit around and wish my life away when I can be doing something new and exciting! Maybe that's why my favorite quote is from Theodore Roosevelt:

"It is not the critic who counts; not the man who points out how the strong man stumbles, or where the doer of deeds could have done them better. The credit belongs to the man who is actually in the arena, whose face is marred by dust and sweat and blood, who strives valiantly; who errs and comes short again and again; because there is not effort without error and shortcomings; but who does actually strive to do the deed; who knows the great enthusiasm, the great devotion, who spends himself in a worth cause, who at the best knows in the end the triumph of high achievement and who at the worst, if he fails, at least he fails while daring greatly. So that his place shall never be with those cold and timid souls who know neither victory nor defeat."

Chapter 26

THE REPAIR PRO

"Fear is like a virus. It can bring an army to its knees in no time."
– Admiral Nimitz

By Dave Kusko & Nancy Irwin

AFTER WORKING IN THE service-and-repair business in both residential and commercial for over 20 years, I'd say that I've serviced and repaired just about everything—air conditioners, furnaces, plumbing and more. I've replaced simple electric outlets to entire circuit boxes. You name it, I've repaired it.

I had been a maintenance supervisor for over 10 years and enjoyed the work, but little by little, I had a whole list of reasons why I hated working for someone else—like the countless times a manager or supervisor got the credit for something I did by myself or with others, and having to train people to be my boss when they had no idea about the industry. And I was so disgusted with the politics and greed of some people that it made me sick. Guess what? I'm not sick anymore!

Finally the day came that I decided to stop having other people feed themselves off of my hard work. At age 47, I felt it was now or never.

I took my years of experience and started my own service-and-repair business. The freedom of having my own time, to pick and choose where I wanted to work and when was, and is, exactly what I wanted.

But with freedom came fear. And I'm not just talking about the fear of failure or fear of success—it's fear of accidents, even death! In my business, I work with natural-gas lines, electricity, torches and the like; and if something goes wrong, who's going to help me? It's different working for someone else; if something goes wrong, you have the safety net of a company to help pay the bills and cover for you, even if it's just for a little while. So when I started my own business, I thought, "Who's going to help me?" Me! But I have to fight that fear. I've always believed that it's how you deal with that fear that makes you succeed or fail.

Another fear that's always in the back of my mind is that no matter how hard or how long I work, I could lose everything. But that's a risk I'm willing to take because I have the drive and commitment inside me to have my own business, play by my own rules and make it all work. I refuse to lose if I can help it.

Before I gave up the security of a steady paycheck, insurance, etc., I talked it over with my dad and my wife and they were behind me 100%. My friends kept asking, "What took you so long?" If it weren't for their encouragement, I'm not sure I'd have had the courage to do this full time.

I tried to go out on my own like this several years ago, but a lot of things just wouldn't come together—I needed more work experience, more business knowledge and more real-world know-how. But here I am a few years later and I've put everything I've learned to good use, and I wouldn't have done it any other way. I'm so focused on my business right now and making it succeed that I can't think that I could lose everything. I keep telling myself, "Be prepared, be creative and be good at whatever it is you will be doing. If and when you do well it all falls back on you, and if you fall on your face, it's you again."

So if you have any doubts or fears about your plans or your future, all I can say is get a grip, make a decision as to what is it you really want, and don't look at what you can possibly lose, but everything you can gain.

Chapter 27

LIFE IS SHORT

"Though 1 walk through the valley 1 will fear not."

– Psalm 23

By Lorraine Guth & Nancy Irwin

AT 79, I WOULD never be mistaken for a baby boomer. But I feel my story of hope, courage and determination could benefit anyone at any age.

I was born on August 20, 1928, in Bridgeport, Connecticut. When I was three months old, my mother was diagnosed with tuberculosis. In those days, people usually died from the disease, so she knew she couldn't care for me properly and signed the adoption papers. I was adopted by a family in Greenwich, Connecticut, at 18 months. My biological mother soon passed away, so her decision had been a wise one. This tragedy left me with many fears as a young child. Before the adoption was finalized, I was placed in one home after another. I remember clinging to my adoptive mother out of fear of losing her, too. This experience is probably what made me so good at overcoming tragedies and obstacles in life.

At the age of 17, I began working as a legal secretary. In the nearly 30 years I stayed in that career, I met and married my husband and raised six children with him. One of my children studied at Vanderbilt University, got his master's from Tennessee University, and is now CEO of 88 mental-health corporations and their facilities. One daughter is a registered nurse, another is a real estate agent and two other daughters are now retired from careers as a mortgage broker and driver's license examiner.

Throughout my own career, I always sought out new and exciting challenges. I worked in advertising as a layout artist for a magazine company in New York City. I worked on the Apollo space program for RCA. In 1971, at the age of 43, I worked in the art department at a furniture company in South Carolina. And from 1973 until 1978, I worked in a law firm for the president of The Florida Bar in Tampa.

And then I decided that I wasn't going to work for somebody else any more. No, I didn't retire—instead, my husband and I, along with our two sons, bought a chemical company. I was the vice president and secretary. We operated the business until my husband passed away in 1990. I needed a change, and it seemed like a good time to get my real estate license, but in the middle of my studies, my son died. Ten days after my son died, I was kidnapped at knifepoint! I helped the police find my attacker and prosecute him. After the perpetrator did his time and got out of prison, I pursued him in civil court and was awarded $3,000! Now he's afraid of me, and that's great because I don't live in a spirit of fear; I trust in the Lord for everything. I had the choice of quitting, staying home and spending my days and nights crying, or staying the course and continuing on with my plans. I decided to disband the chemical company, and at age 62, I moved to Atlanta, bought a home, finished real estate school and got my license.

As you can tell, not much terrifies me—not criminals and certainly not the court system. In fact, in 1994, at age 66, I went back to college and earned a certificate as a private investigator (I use these skills constantly!), and that was just the beginning. Six years later, I enrolled in Georgia State University, where I was on the dean's list numerous times and also inducted into Alpha Lamba Delta National Honor Society. On May 10, 2003, I graduated with a BS in criminal justice at the age of 74! This made the front page in most newspapers across the country that Sunday—which was Mother's Day and a nice present for me!

But I couldn't stop there—I then studied to take the Law School Admission Test so I could enter law school. I passed, and I started classes in Nashville. I had a difficult time in law school—not because of the subject matter or the work, but I had a hard time hearing the professors and was not given a front row seat as I had requested. Under existing disability policies, the school should have honored my request, but it did not. So I had no choice but to leave. I am currently battling the school through the U.S. Justice Department, which now has three pages of disability policies posted in their new catalog. I will return to law school under the provision that I have the preferred seating as I have requested and the courts have mandated. Perhaps my greatest contribution to the law profession will be born from my inability to finish law school!

As you can tell, I am an advocate and refuse to sit back and to take abuse. I wanted my law degree so I could help others, as I have been able to help myself.

I also learned to fly. I bought my first plane in 1968 and my second in 1991. And I've always made room in my life for music, performing and singing; I've been with the Atlanta Country Music Hall of Fame for 14 years and have had the same two managers since 1992. On my 78th birthday I was voted "Entertainer of the Year 2006" by the Atlanta Society of Entertainers. This included all types of music and artists competing from all over Georgia. I was runner-up in the show in 2005. I received the "Gospel Vocalist of The Year" in 2003 and the "Inspiration Award" in 1996. I currently have a gospel radio show on WNAH in Nashville.

Everything in my early life was limiting, but I am an overcomer. If I was told "No," I always heard "Yes." Why? Because I've always enjoyed the challenge. I would rather fail trying than to not try at all.

Even after 80 years, I'm still trying to overcome any and all obstacles. But I keep going because it's better than quitting. And if I had it to do over, I wouldn't change a thing. And if there's one thing I've learned, it's to just go for it and not wait. Wait for what? Time is running out, so you better live life to its full advantage. Even the death of loved ones can make you get up and tackle life instead of sitting around the house feeling sorry for yourself and making yourself sick about it all. I suffer from diabetes, glaucoma, asthma, osteoporosis, thyroid problems, high blood pressure, high cholesterol, arthritis, bad hearing and more! But I take good care of myself. I see my doctors every few months for blood work and checkups. I do what they tell me to do, take what they tell me to take, ask questions if I don't figure out the answers myself and just get on with my life.

Yesterday, I drove 550 miles and then swam non-stop at the YMCA for an hour. Then I cleaned my car and unloaded it and did some work around the house. Today, I mowed the grass and did some heavy housecleaning on both levels of my home. Tomorrow, I leave for New York; I'll be driving 880 miles by myself. Why? Because life is a challenge and I'm always ready and able to meet it.

My story is simply this—you have to have faith and to make the changes and meet the challenges in your life. Never, ever be afraid. And remember that life is short, so embrace your passions and live it up.

Chapter 28

TWO STEPS BACK, THREE STEPS FORWARD

"Think—that this day will never dawn again."

– Dante

By Dave Zagorski, Ph.D.

A S AN APPLIED PSYCHOLOGIST, I've been a jury consultant for just over three years now. In a nutshell, that means that I conduct various kinds of research—from surveys and focus groups to full-scale mock trials—to predict how real-world juries will react in courtroom trials.

Before that, I was a numbers-cruncher in the clothing industry. I hunched over spreadsheets and work orders all day trying to forecast the demand for every possible combination of style, color and size that our firm produced and tried to match production and inventory levels to those projections.

After so many years I'd gotten content and rather complacent in the clothing industry. It certainly wasn't my calling, just an interesting job that I fell into quite accidentally. Suddenly, after I'd been working alongside the same close-knit (no pun intended) and highly entertaining group of colleagues for over a dozen years, we got the news that the owners of our company were planning on shutting the company's doors. Competition from overseas was fierce, and jobs like mine were evaporating quickly in the U.S. Fortunately, we had a year's notice to decide what our next moves would be.

My miniature epiphany came a week after that fateful announcement, during a 10-hour layover in an airport in Bangkok en route to a wedding in India. Faced with all that free time, and without a paperback to distract me, I did what I knew best. I made a spreadsheet. I listed all my strengths and weaknesses, brainstormed about which careers would play to both, and listed what it would take to achieve each of them. I knew that I didn't want to simply chuck all of my quantitative skills out the window but I was yearning to work more closely with the public and to be in a field where I would constantly be learning and evolving. By the time the plane boarded for Delhi, I had decided that I wanted to reinvent myself as a research psychologist. I never looked back after that.

When I researched all the courses involved in meeting the academic requirements, I felt overwhelmed. I already had an MBA but was missing even the most basic prerequisite courses to get into a doctoral program in psychology. So instead of diving right into a Ph.D. program, I had to go back a lot closer to "square one" than I'd planned. I hadn't factored in those extra two years into my brilliant plan or given much thought to how I'd possibly manage to hold down a job while returning to school. It was a classic Homer Simpson "d'oh!" moment.

Because the change involved looking into Ph.D. programs and completing all of the requirements for both a master's and doctoral degree, I was 33 when I committed to the change and 38 when I finally finished.

Once I enrolled in classes and met with an advisor, I was surprised how easy it was to fall back into rhythms of a degree program, and the momentum simply took over. Honestly, the hardest part was looking back wistfully on all those years when I was *only* working a full-time job and had the complete freedom to travel, go to the gym every day, do volunteer projects and spend time with friends. I still worked about 30 hours a week after I returned to school, and while I lamented the loss of my free time, I think that having that "real world" grounding kept me sane.

The biggest fear I faced was how I was going to deal with going into debt in order to make my long-term professional dreams come true. The Catch-22 of being an older student is that once you're out in the work force for a while, financial aid and scholarships are much tougher to come by, because on paper, you don't look needy. My only choice was to sell my condo and use what little equity I'd built up to bridge the gap between my income and my expenses. I agonized over that decision, but going back to renting was the right choice. Even though I ultimately had to take out federal loans for the first two years of my doctoral program (and even dip into my credit cards once or twice just to be able to take a much-needed vacation), I always viewed it as an investment.

I was incredibly fortunate to have a huge support system during those years of metamorphosis. My partner, whom I met during the first year of this process, made sure that no matter how hectic the task of juggling work and school became, we had a harmonious home life and plenty of "no homework allowed" nights to go out and relax.

My bosses were unfailingly supportive and willing to let me adjust my work schedule on the occasions when I couldn't find evening or weekend classes. My friends and family were great about understanding that even though I couldn't accept all of the smaller social invitations, I'd still make it for every birthday and major holiday.

Another unexpected bonus was that my fellow students provided a constant boost. Graduate programs are small and quickly become like extended families, so I always felt that I was being carried along on a current of camaraderie, good humor and genuine friendship.

The money was definitely the toughest obstacle to overcome, although a close runner-up was the six-week "doldrums" that hit me smack dab in the middle of writing my dissertation. I'd already committed to my topic and collected all of my data, but after the distraction of the holidays were over, I suddenly decided that I hated my topic, grew irritable at the stack of statistical print-outs, and abruptly changed the subject any time someone asked me how the project was coming along.

But my goal was always in sight, especially with such a linear process as getting a doctoral degree. There is a very regimented progression from prerequisite courses to the master's degree to electives, and then finally to independent research and working on a dissertation. You always know exactly where you stand and how much more "tunnel" is left until you finally see the light. The funny thing is that, by nature, I'm a procrastinator, so I constantly tricked myself by ratcheting up all of the deadlines. If a paper was due in January, I'd make myself turn it in by Christmas. If a project was due the week of final exams, I'd hoodwink myself by writing in my planner that it was due the week *before* finals.

Without a doubt I would do it all over again—and I'm not promising that I may not get the irresistible urge to make another you-turn in another 10 years or so.

Advice? Make a list of all of the things that you'll have to overcome—both real and imaginary—to achieve your goal. How much time will it take? How much money will it take? Will you need special training? Will you have to move? Will you need to start networking? The most important thing of all is to be very specific about what you'd like to achieve, e.g. "my own shop specializing in South American handicrafts" or "to work full time as a radiologist at Children's Hospital" or "to start a charity that gets medical supplies to war-torn Africa" and by when.

Make sure you don't treat your dream like it's some big, fragile secret that has to be carefully shielded from the light of day. Tell the people closest to you what you'd like to achieve. And don't listen to anyone who says you can't do it. You'll be surprised how many people are willing to help you achieve it, whether it's by offering to watch your kids while you take that weekend real estate course, sticking stamps on the postcards for your band's next gig, or simply by acting as a sounding board.

I admire anyone who, in the process of following their own heart, still manages to find time to enrich the lives of others. I look at people like Jimmy Carter (a strong proponent of Habitat for Humanity) and Dolly Parton (who started a literacy program to bring books to underfunded schools) as perfect examples of this philosophy.

So find someone to admire, to emulate or even copy. And don't worry that you may have to take a couple steps back in order to move forward—that's just part of the journey.

Chapter 29

FOLLOW YOUR BLISS

"I can do all things through Him who strengthens me."
– Philippians 4:13

By Rev. Lisa Graves & Nancy Irwin

THERE I WAS STANDING line with hundreds of other students, waiting and ready to enroll in junior college. As I looked around, I couldn't help but calculate how many years separated me from those around me—could there really be 20 or 25 years' difference in age? I finally reached the little glass partition and gave my name to the administrator who was signing everybody up. She pulled me up on the computer, looked at me and said, "I'm sorry, but you can't carry a full load of classes because you failed the math exam. You will have to take remedial math courses for an entire year and then pass another exam before you can get back on track."

I was devastated and embarrassed. I walked away from the desk, but not from her words, which felt like 1,000 voices yelling "Failure! Failure! Failure!" I stood in the middle of the college cafeteria and began to cry. But somewhere deep inside me I heard another voice, saying "You can do this, don't give up." I went to see the new dean of students, walked into her office and told her, "I have failed the math entrance exam, but I need to carry a full load of courses in order to graduate on time so I can enroll in a four-year college, get into seminary school and graduate by 50." She replied that I could take a full load plus my first of three remedial courses in math, but I'd have to get A's in all my classes to continue doing that. I thanked her, took a full load of classes plus the remedial math (at night) and got straight A's all the way through.

Knowing I could do it carried me forward and increased my courage to not give up. I finally entered seminary at age 47, graduated at 50, was ordained at 52, and at 59 became the solo pastor of a small Presbyterian church (PCUSA) in the mountain town of Clarkesville, in northeast Georgia.

Although I had finally achieved my life's calling, it was a long and arduous road. My second marriage was unraveling. I knew during the tormenting years that this was the second man who would never support my decision to be a minister. It opened my eyes to the reality that I had to be the one to give myself permission to answer God's call on my life.

His was a voice somewhere deep inside of me. A voice that was in the deepest part of my being. In my core. It spoke my name in a way that I knew it knew me. I believe it was God's voice teaching me to recognize my own voice. To trust that voice. To speak. To preach. To never stop.

Even though I knew this was my calling, I still had negative feelings including fear of failure and that I wasn't worthy to be a minister. The biggest obstacle was the sense of failure and lack of self worth due to the sad ending of two marriages and the effect those endings had on my three innocent children. Next was my inner struggle with God's call on my life—not *that* God called me, but *why*. My life had been far from perfect and my mistakes far outnumbered my acts of goodness.

But you know, fear is not such a bad thing. It possesses a lot of energy and power. That energy and power can help you if you can tap into it and redirect it to your advantage. If you stay with it, fear will eventually morph into faith.

In fact, God was (and still is) my biggest cheerleader and the prayers of my family, friends and counselor offered me much love and support.

I always hold in my heart and mind the words of the spiritual activist and author Marianne Williamson:

"Our deepest fear is not that we are inadequate. Our deepest fear is that we are powerful beyond measure. It is our Light, not our Darkness, that most frightens us. You are a child of God. Your playing small does not serve the world. There is nothing enlightening about shrinking so that other people won't feel unsure around you. As we let our own Light shine, we unconsciously give other people permission to do the same. As we are liberated from our own fear, our presence automatically liberates others."

So let go of your fears. Follow your bliss; your passion and the door to the rest of your life will open.

Chapter 30

THE THEORY OF THE COSMIC SLINGSHOT

"The last of the human freedoms is to choose one's attitude
in any given set of circumstances."
– Victor E. Frankl

By Yael Swerdlow

T HERE COMES A TIME in everyone's life when he or she realizes
that their reason for being, their *raison d'etre*, is blocking the
next phase on their life's path. And more often than not, that
realization hurts like hell.

Photojournalism will always be that for me. It was much more than
a career; it was my life, my reason for getting up in the morning, and
I thought I would be doing it forever. I believe with all my heart and

soul in the undefeatable power of truth. And photographs are nothing more than areas of darkness illuminated by points of light.

The only reason I have ever wanted to be a photographer, and the reason I became one, is because I believed if you just show someone, in black and white, images of suffering, people will immediately act unselfishly to right the situation. And I believed *the* way to accomplish this, to save the world, was through pictures, and that this was how I could be of service to humanity, how I could give back and make the world a better place.

I got my heart broken after photographing the aftermath of the genocide in Rwanda in 1994 for International Medical Corps. I had photographs printed up to show all the big magazine editors in New York and D.C.: *TIME, Newsweek, Rolling Stone, Vanity Fair, Fortune, New York Times Magazine, US News and World Report* ... I scheduled three to four interviews per day, every day for a week.

To the magazine editors' dismay, I did not have photographs of the dead: there were no mass graves in my photographs, although I had walked on a few, with bones and bullets dotting the recently tilled earth. Each magazine editor looked at my photographs, not just of the suffering, but of survivors from this genocide that the world chose to ignore. My pictures were not only of man's inhumanity to man, but of man's love and commitment to each other through the efforts of the aid workers, the doctors, the nurses and the volunteers who worked in this hell cleaning up the mess from almost one million dead. Most importantly, I had photographs showing ordinary Rwandans together, doing their best to heal.

I had photographs of the living, of the survivors, of the victims of the world's indifference, of the world's conscience. The editors without exception said my photographs were haunting, but there was no story, so it was *so* over. The only thing the world wants to know about is the latest OJ Simpson development.

In her office, the photo editor for the *Atlantic Monthly* was more than annoyed at my photographs. She flipped through them as if looking at ads in a magazine, finally slamming my portfolio book shut exasperatedly, and said, "Nobody cares about Rwanda, okay? Don't you have any photographs of rich kids growing up in Bel Air????"

I felt my heart break. But she was right.

And now, more than a dozen years later, after all the Rwandan movies and hand wringing, and apologies, there have been at least half a dozen genocides around the world, with thousands and thousands of photographs of man's inhumanity to man recording all of it. Still, we look at the photographs and then watch Larry King interview Paris Hilton.

Not willing to completely leave the journalism field, I took a job on the other side of the desk as the director of media relations, Consulate General of Israel in Los Angeles. It was ironic, because as a photojournalist I had consciously avoided working in the Middle East, as had many of my colleagues. Our rationale was simple: we only wanted to work on stories with an ending in sight—wars and famines do end at some point. We all knew the Israeli-Arab conflict was endless misery. Photojournalists hate to work in futile situations because it means our photographs don't have any power.

While working at the Israeli Consulate, it became painfully clear I am much more skilled at conflict resolution when I do not have to adhere to official government statements and officially stated positions. To be sure, conflict resolution was not in my job description, but it was, in my mind and heart, the sole reason I accepted the position. And in this situation, one of the most volatile and divisive issues in the world, I needed to have the freedom to speak from my heart while not compromising the position of those whom I had been hired to represent.

Therefore, I decided to get my master's degree in a field in which I could ascend to the next level in making the world a better place: the newly created master's in public diplomacy at the University of Southern California, the very first such program in the world.

Overcoming negative beliefs was difficult. I was so exhausted and demoralized by the time I left the Israeli Consulate. My experiences from photojournalism had piled up on top of my consulate experiences, as well as other traumas. So, I not only had to find my belief in myself again, but I also had to rediscover my faith in the world and its goodness. With each of those careers, I was always on high alert. I was also in a constant siege mentality, with fight-or-flight my only instinct. I was a mess, even sleeping in the fetal position.

On a more practical level, I had to learn how to be a student again to regain my study habits, to know I could pass exams (especially the GRE) and to write papers. Most importantly, I had to accept that going back to college at almost 50 years old was not a completely insane idea.

"Why bother" was insidiously looping through my head, so I knew that my mental programming had to change. Hypnotherapy did the trick. First, I tackled passing the graduate entrance exam, which took a few sessions over a few weeks. Then I moved on to finding my voice again, resetting my compass, getting myself back. That took almost a year of twice-monthly therapy sessions.

My most immediate fear was of math and of taking exams in general. Once I got the test out of the way, I began to really examine and exorcise the negative thought patterns that had put those messages in my head in the first place. This led to an incredible cleansing of damaging thought patterns that had held me back in the most important aspects in my life.

My best friends were very supportive, but it didn't matter much when I was trying to counter the negative thoughts and emotions in my head. I felt very alone and isolated, and therapy opened up the door to light.

Mostly, I had to accept that what I was attempting mattered, that I mattered, and that my goals were worth it—that I am worth it.

By far the hardest part was I had to admit to myself that I have never been content to be just the photographer. We still bear witness to the rough draft of history, but for all the belief I had in the power of the medium, it became agonizingly clear how neutered that power could be, and I couldn't stand it. It's why I've always had to move on. But now, I had to find that place inside me that believed I could still make a difference, with or without my cameras.

Underneath all my fears, however, I am blessed with an "f-you," never-say-die attitude toward criticism. I'm also blessed with a circle of great friends and family and a therapist who disconnected the negative voices and pumped up the volume of the positive ones.

I honestly don't know what my future holds other than it will call on all my talents: writing, photography and building bridges between people. I know it will be focused around my passion for bringing light into darkness and working toward the greater good. And that's all that matters to me.

This is where the hypnotherapy really has worked—I am much calmer and more open to options (and for a control freak, that is pretty amazing in and of itself). My faith in the grand scheme is solid now.

My only advice to those who are considering making a transition in midlife is to not look back. And if you find yourself in that fearful stage, just believe that personal courage is the flower among the weeds. You have to make sure it does not get strangled.

This is "the theory of the cosmic slingshot" and I am living it (and to celebrate it, I have created the "cosmic slingshot martini"), which is:

You think you are living the life you are destined to live: in the job or career you're meant to have, in the relationship with the person you're destined to be with for the rest of your life, in the location you're supposed to live in, and you are sure in your gut your life is exactly what is meant for you. And then something happens, and you are flung—literally, or emotionally, or physically, or spiritually, or psychically—unceremoniously and sometimes harshly, to the opposite end of the universe. You land hard but you pick yourself up, dust yourself off and realize *that's* where you're supposed to be, doing what you're truly meant to be doing, with the person you're really meant to be with, in the location where you're meant to live.

I truly believe that if you are in tune with yourself and can quiet down enough to listen to your soul, there will be more than one cosmic slingshot in your life. And of course, it's meant to be shaken, not stirred.

Chapter 31

KICK YOUR DOUBTS IN THE TEETH

"I'd rather die on my feet than live on my knees."
– Unknown

By Mack Reed & Nancy Irwin

HAD BEEN A REPORTER for over 15 years, but by 1997 the newspaper industry was (and still is) dying. I had made it as far as covering Ventura County—a sleepy, rural town north of LA—for the *Los Angeles Times*. Getting burned out on a steady diet of small-town news, I was desperate to find something else to do, and the day came when I hit the proverbial wall. I wanted to cover the news in LA.

But competition in the journalism field is stiff and as rigid as plate-steel. And with only one or two jobs opening up each year —and those always going to a Pulitzer Prize winner, literary lion or other unassailable genius—my chances were slim to none.

My dream of being a reporter on a major metropolitan daily permeated every thought, and I felt that anything less than pure journalism was beneath me. I had this weird preconceived notion that I was born to live my dream and attain my dream job, and that everyone standing in my way simply couldn't see it.

I underwent a short course of therapy to examine my general misery at the situation and found that I had wrapped up too much of my self-esteem, and thus my sense of equilibrium, in my job. In other words, without the "right" job, I was no one and therefore, miserable. About ten sessions persuaded me otherwise—and, at the age of 41, I discovered that it was entirely within *my* power to change my beliefs about my situation.

By now, I had already begun dabbling in HTML and had built myself a solid little website. When the want ad popped up in the *LA Times* itself—for a major web-portal network that needed a news producer for a new site in Orange County—I jumped on it.

My family and my wife had long tired of me whining about how miserable newspapering was making me, so they applauded my decision to enter therapy and supported my search for work in multimedia/online.

At the time, one of my biggest fears was that my boss would find out I was looking and somehow ruin the opportunity for me. I also feared that the new gig would somehow evaporate—this was '97, well before the dot-com boom/bust, when the internet was all new-fangled. And I feared (a bit) that journalism on the web was not "legit" enough, and that I'd lose whatever stature the world accorded me for being a "big-city newspaper journalist."

I also was fearful of the internet world and that because I was not *of* that world, I couldn't be welcomed by it. And I harbored fear that I was walking away from the one true calling I'd always had. When I found myself stuck in that fearful stage, I just kept asking myself, "Do you really want to spend the rest of your life wishing and wondering?"

And in the words of Goethe (well, the quote is widely attributed to Goethe but it's not really his):

"Until one is committed, there is hesitancy, the chance to draw back—concerning all acts of initiative (and creation), there is one elementary truth that ignorance of which kills countless ideas and splendid plans: that the moment one definitely commits oneself, then Providence moves too. All sorts of things occur to help one that would never otherwise have occurred. A whole stream of events issues from the decision, raising in one's favor all manner of unforeseen incidents and meetings and material assistance, which no man could have dreamed would have come his way. Whatever you can do, or dream you can do, begin it. Boldness has genius, power and magic in it. Begin it now."

In other words, I told myself, "Don't be a wuss. Quick, before you lose your nerve: GO. NOW." My favorite heroes, I'd have to say, are the Renaissance men— Leonardo DaVinci, Buckmeister Fuller, Ben Franklin, Dean Kamen, Buckaroo Banzai—so I imagined myself a true Renaissance man. I devised my own lesson plan and how to get started and get out, which worked well for me and might work for others: if anyone's faced with a midlife transition, my only advice is, don't wait! Kick your doubts in the teeth! Make that leap of faith! You have no idea what's on the other side of the crevasse, but if you don't leap, you'll never know. Say you're going to do it, promise yourself you're going to do it, and the second you make that promise, think, "What's my next step?" Continue identifying next steps and take them.

Lack skills? Get them. Beg, borrow or steal to educate yourself so you can have that one line on your resume that's missing. What skills do you have to trade to someone who can teach you? Barter.

One thing's for sure—you're not going anywhere sitting on your ass.

Chapter 32

NEVER TOO LATE

"Damn the torpedoes, full speed ahead!"
– Admiral David Glasgow Farragut

By Anne Grimm & Nancy Irwin

I'M AN 80-YEAR-OLD GREAT-GRANDMOTHER who was a victim of domestic abuse for 47 years.

My children still can't believe that "dear old Dad" could have caused any problems for me. They wouldn't believe that I'm finally free of fear only since seeing his death certificate—even though he was remarried and living in another state 2,500 miles away, dying at last in a nursing home. (I still did not feel safe until I saw the death certificate needed by Social Security.)

A product of the Great Depression and World War II, I never had a choice of what to do with my life. We didn't have any laws to protect women in abusive relationships back then, and only in recent years have things gotten better. Some women are still victimized by the courts, attorneys and the law, despite the strides that have been made in recent decades.

In my day, women couldn't count on any kind of support system, and for me divorce was out of the question. But now there are agencies out there that can help women and their children, and it's never too late to turn around on that road you're traveling, take your life into your hands and leave any kind of abusive relationship.

After 15 years of bruises, cuts and scrapes from engineered "accidents," I had a nervous breakdown and tried to check myself into the mental hospital. I was told by the female interviewer at that facility that I had not lost touch with reality, but to go back to the family doctor and arrange for counseling. Then I was advised by a (male) counselor, "Why don't you just do what your husband tells you to?" As though I hadn't been doing that all along. No, people just didn't understand back then, not even health professionals or law enforcement.

Even at the end when I escaped, no one believed my plea for help in the doctor's office, and I was advised to go home with him and to seek counseling. My desperation finally was recognized when I insisted that I would instead break windows or do whatever damage was necessary to get me taken to jail or the state mental hospital. From there, the process put me into the domestic violence shelter.

After 47 years and nearly four months, I had no choice but to leave. I had to file for divorce—I couldn't go back no matter how he pleaded. My life depended on escape. To help others make the safe choice, I developed the website for DAWN (Domestic Abuse Women's Net): www.WillapaChapterDawn.org. In addition to my own mistreatment by my husband, he also lied to others about me to save face while I was hiding in the domestic violence shelter. To make matters worse, my civil rights were violated by inept government personnel in charge of providing law-decreed pension and survivor benefits, as well as by the lawyers and courts who refused me consideration.

Here are a few facts you should know:

• Every nine seconds in the United States, a woman is assaulted and beaten.

• Every day, four women are murdered by boyfriends or husbands.

• Women are most likely to be killed when attempting to leave their abuser. In fact, they're at a 75% higher risk than those who stay.

Battered-woman syndrome involves four psychological stages: denial, guilt, enlightenment, responsibility. I went through all four, being finally forced by the ultimate fear into the last. There are four forms of battering:

• **Physical**–includes pushing, shoving, slapping, hitting with fist, kicking, choking, grabbing, pinching, pulling hair or threatening with weapons.

• **Sexual**–includes forced sex with the threat of violence, sex after violence has occurred or the use of objects or damaging acts without the woman's consent.

• **Psychological/Emotional**–includes brainwashing, control of the woman's freedom to come and go when she chooses, blocking access to members of her childhood family. May also include staging "accidents" to set up a reason to verbally abuse the victim as inept, awkward, stupid.

• **Destruction of property or pets.**

Even though I'm 80 years old, I'm committed to educating women and releasing them from fear. What is there to be afraid of, especially if you have no choice but to go ahead? What? He cannot kill you more than once. Even living in a wheelchair is better than death. I stayed as long as I did because I could hold my own, living with the tension, without others' knowing. I left only when no choice remained.

Finally free in having outlived him, I'm very relaxed and happy in my old age. I'm content in all the hard work and misery I went through to achieve the goal of "becoming an ancestor." But more than that, I lead a delightfully fruitful life in other ways. I've had five books published since he has been gone; a sixth will be published very soon and I am writing my seventh—a book of children's stories—for publication in 2008.

You can do it, too. Be happy again, and free.

Chapter 33

JUST GETTING STARTED

"I take nothing for granted. I now have only good days, or great days."

– Lance Armstrong

By Jacques Soriano & Nancy Irwin

FOR 25 YEARS I made a fantastic living as an executive sales director and provided a comfortable life for myself and my family. But it was always by working for *other* people and *other* companies ... making *their* dreams come true.

While attending Chellie Campbell's Financial Stress Reduction Workshop, I realized that only I could determine my destiny in life and in my professional career. I decided to stop putting a ton of money into my employer's pocket and start my own firm.

Four months after I turned 45, I made the commitment to start my own business, Soriano & Associates, a direct marketing firm that predominantly serves medium-size businesses and non-profit organizations. So far it's been the best decision I've ever made in my professional career. Even though it was scary, as I had a young family to provide for, I just had to take the risk. Marcia Wieder says, "You can change your beliefs so they empower your dreams and desires. Create a strong belief in yourself and what you want." So between Marcia and Chellie, I was able to overcome almost immediately my previous fear of failure. I realized that it was my own internal fears that were stopping me, and I was the one who had created them! I figured I could replace them with faith in myself and my business.

The business is still in the start-up phase, but I'm excited for the future. Of course, while the business gets going and gets growing, it is somewhat of a struggle financially for my family and me, but this chance will pay off big in the long term. My wife and kids have been extremely supportive, and if I had to do this all over again, I'd do it in a heartbeat. Absolutely! I feel it's important to make changes no matter *what* stage of your life you happen to be in, as long as you are passionate about it and committed to making it work.

It's extraordinarily fulfilling. I'm the boss now, and I'm certain that the day will come when I'll be putting a whole lot of money in MY pockets!

Chapter 34

ALEIKUM SALAAM WA RAHMAT ALLAH WA KARAKATU

("Upon you be peace and the mercy of God and his blessing")
"There came a time when the risk to remain tight in the bud
was more painful than the risk it took to blossom."

– Anais Nin

By Tracy Karbus & Nancy Irwin

IN 2001, I STARTED waking up angry every morning. I allowed this to go on for 24 months as I struggled with giving up all the external securities I had created for myself over a period of 14 years. One day I knew I'd had enough. I was done with this behavior. I had been living in Washington state for the past decade and a half, and decided to close my successful business, sell my house and move back to the place I was born and raised. At the time I was married, and my husband and I both agreed that this would be an important move for us. Once we moved back to Southern California, I took the whole year off to search my soul for the next journey in my life. I was challenged by this decision more than once during that year, being lured by opportunities that would put me back on the financial treadmill of life and relieve any fears I had about not having enough money (even though I had been very responsible financially in allowing for this sojourn).

These opportunities only caught my attention for a fleeting moment, as my gut told me to hold out and trust the commitment I had made to myself. That was the hardest thing for me to do, but it paid off, especially since I felt so strongly that I needed to take a detour. I was living a life focused outwardly on the opinions of others, and I could feel the life energy slowly leaving my body. My creativity was shutting down and I felt no joy in my life. I thought this was how everybody lived life and it was normal. I had the choice to continue that pattern or respond to the parts of myself that felt as if they were dying. Finally, I didn't care what normal was, and I made a commitment to myself to change my situation because I was filled with energy and knew my life was meant for greater things. I ended the year off by running a marathon. I learned from that experience that my mind ran the marathon and my body followed. It was a pivotal point in my life because I knew that I could do just about anything I set my mind to after running 26.2 miles.

The following year, I became regional director for a non-profit that supported women developing entrepreneurial opportunities. This position challenged every part of me while it ignited my passion for understanding women and their belief systems. I remained in that position for close to three years, when I came to what I believed to be one of the big turning points in my life.

At the beginning of 2004, I decided to leave my director position and travel somewhere I had never been before. I picked up brochures, travel magazines, anything I could get my hands on to find that just-right destination—but I couldn't find it. So then I decided to give up the search and let it find me. The following month I went out to the Mojave Desert to help a friend put on a 100-mile endurance horse race. I updated her on my life, "idling in neutral" as it seemed, and told her I wanted to travel. She mentioned she had been invited to Egypt to assist in managing a horse race and asked me to come along to work with her. I knew in that moment that this was *the* travel opportunity I had been searching for.

Within eight days, we were landing in Cairo. Our plan was to visit for 10 days and then return home. That amazing journey was filled with horses, adventure and warm Egyptian hospitality. However, it was also 10 days too short for me. I had the time, the boldness and the means to extend my trip. And extend my trip I did. "When will you be back?" my husband asked. "I'm not sure, but I'm sure it won't be that long," I answered.

A trusted Egyptian friend put me touch with a local Bedouin, with whom I trekked the Sinai Desert—along with his "camel in training" that carried our food, water and bedding. We traveled for three days and two nights, and moved at a rhythm that allowed the body the least amount of resistance or expenditure of energy. As I kept his silhouette in the corner of my eye, I walked in complete freedom from thought. It seemed as if I was gliding over the sands of the desert in meditation. There was lightness to my body that enabled me to walk from sunrise until sunset without fatigue. At the end of the third day, I sauntered back into base camp behind my guide and his camel. Something was different with me however. I can't specify when the "aha" moment came on this three-day journey, but I knew that I returned filled with a strong measure of peace within and the courage to end my marriage.

I was 44 years old, but this was the start of a rebirth.

I remained in the countryside (approximately 20 minutes south of the Giza Pyramids) for the duration of my trip as I allowed myself to sit with the feeling of not knowing what to do next. I lived each day connected to my surroundings and decided that I would know when the time was right for me to leave. The trust in that knowing brought me back to the United States 67 days later. I was not by any means returning as that same woman who left over two months earlier. I was in the 17th year of my marriage when I departed on this journey, and I also knew down to the roots of my soul that this marriage was the one "untruth" in my life. It was time to release my husband and myself from a relationship that was not working for either of us. We decided to divorce. We had been struggling for years and did not know when and how to end it, but as one friend said, "ending a relationship can be compared to a fruit ripening on a tree; when it is at its full maturity, it will drop off the limb." We separated all our belongings, cried over the love that was still between us and agreed to remain friends. The house we lived in sold right away and within eight weeks I was on my way back to Egypt for an infinite period of time.

I arrived in Cairo during the mid-summer heat. I didn't really have any expectations about what the future would hold and learned to stay in the moment as I entered a time in my life when self-reflection and observation exposed many of my truths from within. I learned that I was carrying around guilt about ending the relationship even though it was the right thing to do. I became angry at all I had given up for the needs of others over the years. I felt as if I had abandoned myself. Finally, I went through a grieving process that took me through places of heart-breaking sorrow and belly-aching laughter. For the first time in my life, I was alone and relieved of the duties of nurturer and giver. This led me to become keenly connected to my core beliefs and wants.

I chose to live in the countryside of lower Egypt, among Egyptians who were mostly illiterate and worked the land as a means of survival. These were people of tradition and a strong sense of community and family. Rush-hour traffic consisted of dodging flocks of sheep, donkey carts and gamossa (water buffalo) crossings. I did not speak much Arabic, so for the first time in my life I was mostly silent. I had to trust my judgment (partly as a survival mechanism) in reading the tones, body language and energy of the people before me. It helped me to gauge when and how to interact. There were moments of rumblings or feelings of unease that erupted in my gut that I needed to acknowledge—a guide that I'd had all my life but have only learned to unquestionably trust since Egypt.

Each day took me down a path leading to greater self-knowledge as I learned to live among these very sensitive people. There were moments when I felt as if my self-confidence was being undermined, and I became confused and frustrated. For quite some time I believed some of the "opinions" and "helpful advice" friends offered to me and neglected to trust my instincts when something did not feel right. Day after day brought me face to face with the opportunity to examine what I believed in, who deserved my trust and what was negotiable.

After a good year and a half, I felt ready to make a more permanent commitment to my life in Egypt. I did a lot of research and decided to make an investment in the local real estate market. With the help of the locals, I secured land and built a modest house for myself in Sakkara, a village on the outskirts of Cairo. I referred to this house as my temple. It was here that I sat with the fear of loneliness—only to discover that I was great company and I actually enjoyed my humor and sensitivities. As I became grounded in my sense of self, I connected with my femininity, wisdom and what it really meant to be a woman in all of her essence and beauty. I also learned to redefine "home" as that wonderfully divine place within my heart that travels with me where ever I might live. That home is not always a physical place, but an accumulation of life experiences gained from testing the water, taking risks and living amongst all of the earth. It is a place of self-knowledge, compassion, understanding, wisdom, courage and gratitude, and it guides me every day.

It was also here that I came full circle; three years after leaving California for Egypt, that I made the decision to go back to where my family and friends lived. So in the winter of 2007, I sold my house in Sakkara to a family from the UK and moved my personal belongings back to California.

Life has taught me to hold a very strong trust in the fact that I am being guided, thus the very strong inner knowing that I was supposed to be in Egypt for that period of time in my life. Ultimately it was the belief in myself to make the best decisions possible that allowed me to move freely in and out of daily life and sometimes difficult situations.

People often ask me, "What made you go there?" My answer is always the same. I needed to be in a place where I was anonymous. Where nobody wanted to give me advice or judge me. Where I also felt a sense of ease to discover life and what I wanted. A place where I could get on a horse and ride until I was saddle sore and nobody cared. Finally, I think that Egypt had been on my radar screen for many years. My eldest brother reminded me that for as long as he could remember, I was always looking at books about the pyramids. Since I believe that to which we give energy becomes reality, I therefore know I had been working on this one for a long time.

I've always depended solely on myself, but I've found that to be a very boring mantra to live by. I've developed a small network of confidants that help to carry some of the unnecessary weight I have been known to impose on myself. I also believe that it is equally important to be courageous and generous in spirit to the callings of the heart and mind. Not searching for approval from others and *always* doing my homework. Because we always know more than we give ourselves credit for—the importance of identifying what is negotiable and what is not and *sticking to it* has been one of my greatest learnings. Finally, as Maya Angelou always said, "When someone tells you who they are, believe them."

I departed Egypt knowing that I had been privileged to experience greater depths of love, introspect, maturity and compassion for life.

When I returned to the States, I felt rejuvenated enough to start my consulting company, The Fifth aElement LLC, based on the idea that aether (also called quintessence, from quinta essentia, "fifth element") is the element that holds the power of life—it also can be defined as pure energy whose force is imagined to be like lightning. This ideology is the underlying theme I utilize in developing people, ideas and opportunities.

Without the clear understanding of what I discovered about myself and how to harness my energy, I don't know if I could have been as successful or as satisfied as I have become.

You don't have to travel all the way to Egypt to discover the hidden potential in yourself; just know and trust that forces of powerful change reside within you.

Chapter 35

A LITTLE MUSIC, A LOT OF LOVE

"Walk through fear—there's happiness on the other side."
– Unknown

By Gary Larkin & Nancy Irwin

O N FEBRUARY 9, 1964, an estimated 73 million people were watching The Beatles perform on *The Ed Sullivan Show*. I was one of them. From that moment on, my dream was to be a musician. Starting in the 7th grade and all through high school, I performed in a number of rock 'n' roll bands.

When it was time to go off to college, I really didn't think about the music anymore. That's what you do, right? You grow up, go to college and do something with your life. So I got a degree in education, got a job teaching high school, got a wife, and then I asked, "Hey! What about my music?" So, in 1978, the two of us left our home in New York and traveled to Los Angeles, where I was more than determined to live my dream and be a successful songwriter and musician.

While I performed at night, I held a variety of day jobs to pay the bills—telemarketer, singing waiter and even touring as a stand-up comic. But after so many years and too many rejections, both in music and telemarketing, I just couldn't bear to hear the word "no" one more time.

It was around this time that I became a father. My wife and I adopted a baby boy from Korea, and I had made up my mind that I didn't want to call him from a phone booth in Podunk one day to say "happy birthday." But I was at a loss as to what to do with my life. I called out to the cosmos, to God, "Help me! I'll do whatever you want."

Then one day there was an ad in the paper for a teacher at The Optimists' Children's Home, a division of Optimists International, to work with the county and state in placing gang kids on probation in detention. So there I was, acting like a grown-up again and teaching English, math and science to a roomful of gang-bangers.

But it felt different this time. I now had a son who needed me. Hunter was a very sweet and very silent little boy who displayed extraordinary abilities. He learned the alphabet from *Sesame Street*, then proceeded to memorize the words he saw on the screen. He could spell an amazing number of words using his magnetic letters on the floor. He had a special love of baseball videos and could spell the names of all the Dodgers (both Brooklyn and LA), complete with batting averages! However, he could hardly speak by 3 and a half, and could not tolerate many sounds that most people consider normal, along with many forms of touch. Haircuts were torture, and he had no way of telling us other than to scream.

He was diagnosed with autism, a disturbance in psychological development in which the use of language, reaction to stimuli, interpretation of the world and formation of relationships are not fully established and follow unusual patterns. That's the dictionary's definition. But all my wife and I knew was that we loved our little boy and wanted to find answers and programs that could help him.

Our journey on the maze of "services" began after he was enrolled in a special education preschool program. Over the years, we had made it our business to learn everything we could about autism and the services available (although not readily available without a fight), to children like our son. The Los Angeles Unified School District has always been, and continues to be, reluctant (to put it mildly!) to pay for "extra" services. The services Hunter has received have all been ones that we brought to the attention of the school district. We retained an attorney who acted as our advocate. We have been through mediation and arbitration with the school system over an educational therapist (who turned out to be Hunter's own "Annie Sullivan" by giving him language). Ironically, the school district was responsible for our legal fees when the attorney had to be called in to fight for us! We fought for speech and occupational therapies, both school- and clinic-based, and won! We had even secured funding from the school district for Fast Forward, a computer-based language program, and for Auditory Integration Training, now referred to as Digital Auditory Aerobics, along with his current non-public-school placement!

After fighting nonstop for my son, I knew that I had to get the message out there to other parents. After working as a special education teacher for over 20 years, having earned both an MA and MS degree from National University, I earned my Marriage Family Therapist License, specializing in special-needs children and their families.

Through the work I've undertaken on behalf of my son, I've embarked on a whole new career. I teach a class on "mainstreaming" in the teacher credential program at various colleges, while also teaching at John Marshall High School in Los Angeles. In addition, I'm a family therapist for the adoption department of 5 Acres in Pasadena, and have also taught at UCLA Extension, the University of South Dakota, and the University of Phoenix. I've become an expert on special-education law, classroom modifications, program accommodations and learning disabilities. I now have a private educational therapy practice in which I provide treatments such as digital auditory aerobics, I consult with schools on ways to best serve the special-needs child in the general education classroom, and I act as an advocate for these children and their families at individual education-planning meetings. And I'm currently in the process of writing a book to assist these families in accessing the necessary services, self-help and support.

OK, so maybe I'm not the rock 'n' roll star I dreamed I'd be, but I still have my music—and a loving family, and a house full of Beatles memorabilia. Here's how I see it: if music's supposed to change the world or how you see that world, then maybe what I'm doing—working as an advocate for disabled kids and their families—has helped the world, too.

As much as I admire the words and works of John Lennon, Thomas Edison, Swami Swahananda and Mickey Larkin (my dad), the words of Father Flanagan of Boys Town always encourage me: "No man stands tall as when he bends to help a child."

Yeah, yeah, yeah.

Chapter 36

ESCAPING THE DESK

"Friends are the family you choose for yourself."

– Anonymous

By Ellen Grosser & Nancy Irwin

HAVE YOU EVER FELT like you're being held prisoner, but instead of jail, you're shackled to your desk? If you've ever hated working for someone else, you know what I'm talking about. I felt imprisoned just by the fact I was working for someone else. My time was not my own. I had to show up on time and stay all day until quitting time even if there was nothing for me to do. My last job in "prison" was at an infomercial company sourcing new products. It wasn't "me," and it sucked. And just like anything trapped inside a cage, all that matters to you is freedom. So I escaped.

A job as a real estate agent, I thought, would be an ideal one for me. I love people and houses and best of all, I'd love working for myself. The only problem I could foresee was the lack of a regular paycheck. It was scary to think about—the only way to earn money was to go out and make it happen. An unsteady income was just one of the fears I had to overcome. I was scared I would fail the licensing exam, and that I wouldn't be able to make a living from real estate. I knew the test would be very difficult for me—was over 50 years old and had never been a good student. I struggled to memorize all that information, and I was also required to use a lot of math—another poor subject for me. But instead of drowning in negativity, I decided to change my mental "programming" to a positive one. It took a few months, but I did it.

My husband was very supportive of my plans and all the work I was putting into them. Believe it or not, my husband's ex-wife was visiting our area at the time and actually helped me with the math. Even with all the supportive peers around me, it was my baby granddaughter who really kept me going. I was determined to have a job where I had free time to spend with her on a regular basis, and I wanted money to buy her things and help send her to private school.

It was extremely hard work, but if I had to do it over again, I would. The benefits of doing what I love are immeasurable.

People ask me, "Who are your role models?" I'd have to say, "Me!" My family never really had any successful females, and I always had to fend for myself. So I'm especially proud of my decisions and success.

Are you thinking about making a transition in midlife or already in the process? My advice to you is to have faith and believe in yourself. Just stay positive and optimistic, because it makes life a lot easier. And remember, you CAN do it!

Escaping the Desk

Chapter 37

MAN ON FIRE

"If you can talk with crowds and keep your virtue,
Or walk with kings—nor lose the common touch,
If neither foes nor loving friends can hurt you;
If all men count with you, but none too much,
If you can fill the unforgiving minute
With sixty seconds' worth of distance run,
Yours is the Earth and everything that's in it,
And—which is more—you'll be a Man, my son!"
– Rudyard Kipling

By Stan Davis & Nancy Irwin

THE FLAMES LURCHED SEVERAL feet up into the air; smoke billowed out in swells of black and gray. I only had enough time to grab half of my belongings before the fire fully engulfed my car. As I stood on the corner of Martin Luther King Jr. Boulevard at Crenshaw, near the USC campus, crowds gathered and watched as the fire department arrived and doused my totally burned-out car.

It was my first day in Los Angeles.

I was well into my 30s and newly divorced, and I had traveled over 1,300 miles from a little town called Denton, Texas, to come to LA and pursue my dreams of being an actor. I'd left a radio show DJ position there to do so.

Had all my dreams gone up in smoke? No, only my material possessions. But it was a defining moment in my life. I could have turned around, gone back home and returned to the life as a sales account executive. But I couldn't. I wouldn't. I had a fire burning in me and nothing was going to put it out. I stayed in LA.

But after that first rush of "Yeah, I'm gonna do it" adrenaline hit me, I was left with the fear of, how can I act and eat at the same time? I worked at a variety of jobs—security guard, marketing, cell-phone salesman. By day, I climbed the ladder to become the No. 1 sales person and by night, I was learning my timing and everything at a comedy workshop, which later led me to The Groundlings, an improvisational theater troupe in LA. Next thing you know, I'm doing stand-up at The Comedy Store. I had the desire to be a serious actor, too, but success was slow and I wasn't getting the breaks.

People said, "Give up. Do it as a hobby." But I never believed in that. I felt that making $50,000 as a cell phone salesman was the hobby. That helped pay the rent, but acting was my true calling.

Even as a kid, I always wanted to entertain people. I remember walking into a movie theater and seeing people's heads as big as a building on a screen, and I saw the emotional effect it had on the audience. Even though I was only 5 or 6 at the time, I knew that performing was what I wanted to do with my life.

So I stuck it out. I never gave up—I'm not built that way and I wasn't raised that way. My grandmother Josie instilled in me that "I can do anything if I put my mind to it" spirit. She was a smart, elegant lady who helped shape me and bestowed upon me the gift of having to work for what I wanted. If there was something that I needed or wanted, she'd always tell me to make half of the money and she would pay the other half. That was the best thing she could have done. So starting when I was 5, I had a paper route for a few years. Later, I worked for the pharmacist at the corner store. Not only did she let me know that I could have everything I ever wanted, but that I deserved it, too.

Grandma Josie also taught me that we all choose our own paths, and she gave me a road map to education, honesty, responsibility and courtesy. I still say "yes, ma'am" and "no, ma'am" to my elders, and "thank you" is an automatic reflex. All my grandparents were the first generation in my family to live a life out of slavery, and they wanted to make their children's and grandchildren's lives better than they could ever imagine. So I make sure that I live my life in honor.

I was hit by a car when I was 11 years old. The doctors told me that I would never walk again, and my family, especially my grandmother, refused to believe it. She would visit me in the hospital every day and talk to me and rub my legs and tell me that someday I would walk out of the hospital. And I did. I have that determined spirit that says nothing's going to keep me down. Guess I learned literally that when you get knocked down, you just get back up and move on.

So I kept at it and kept my dreams alive. I got an agent and, being at the right place at the right time, things started happening. Then I got my first real acting job, and I've been working steadily every since. I've made it seven years and still haven't had to go back to the 9 to 5 sales job. Acting is now my real job. My career has supported my life, and if you call that being a successful actor, then I am a successful actor. It's what *I* call a success. That all kicked in when I was about 47—so I guess you can call me a 15-year overnight success.

I've been in a lot of movies, including *Primary Colors* with John Travolta, *City of Angels* with Meg Ryan and Nicholas Cage, and by the time this book comes out, so will my new movie, *The Adventures of Beatle Boyin*. I've also appeared in dozens of TV shows—*Desperate Housewives*, *Lincoln Heights*, *The Closer*, *My Name Is Earl* and many others—plus commercials and voiceovers.

With all my good fortune, I think it's important to give back. One thing I'm always reminded of, and I always share with people, is Mother Theresa's philosophy—she said that she woke up every day and saw God in everybody and every living thing. Not from a religious place, but seeing every human being as something that came from creation; that there is good in every person. So I try to give back by coaching and teaching other actors and encouraging them not give in to the negative or the I-can'ts or the I-never–wills because as soon as you do, you fail.

Hollywood, being Hollywood, however, has thrown a few obstacles my way—ageism and racism, just to name a couple. But these are obstacles I'm determined to overcome because I believe that I have talent; I have something valuable to offer and I will make it. You can't let a few obstacles get in the way of your dreams. In many ways, dreams are all we have.

My cousin gave me the book *The Alchemist* by Paulo Coelho, and it's the story of a little boy who sets out to follow his dreams but becomes fearful. "My heart is afraid of what I'll have to suffer," he says. The alchemist replies, "Tell your heart that the fear of suffering is worse than the suffering itself. And that no heart has ever suffered when it goes in search of its dreams."

If you have a dream, and it's something you truly desire, and you take that first step, you've already started down the path toward realizing that dream; you're on your way to success. What's the alternative? You sit around and talk about your dreams until you're 50 or 60 years old and full of regrets like "I wish I hadn't done that," "I wish I had done this," "I wish I hadn't married her, "I wish I didn't have a 9 to 5 job" or worse, "I wonder what would've happened if I hadn't quit."

I've always believed that if you can deal with all of the adversity that the world throws at you—fame or failure—then you're a success. Just learn to be steady. I've had to walk that fine line between ego and low self-esteem. Self-esteem runs out a lot—especially in Los Angeles—and that's a daily challenge. I have moments when I feel so overwhelmed that I don't know what I'm going to do, but I pull myself up and the next thing I know, I'm on the other side of it and realize it's not that bad.

I really don't have any fears—acting makes you fearless. Stanislavsky once said, "Acting is real behavior in imaginary circumstances." He didn't say if it was real "young" behavior, or real "woman" behavior or real "white" behavior, but how we as human beings behave from the womb until we die. If Hollywood was true to the human condition or human experiences, then I should have no fear of getting older. So I'm enjoying myself. I try not to call negative things to me, or be a victim. It's about me doing what I'm supposed to be doing 24/7.

God, or the universe, whatever the power is that runs everything, put me where I'm supposed to be and everything around me supports what it is I'm supposed to be doing.

On the drive out here through Texas, New Mexico, Arizona and California, I envisioned the kind of life I wanted for myself—and now I'm living it, as a successful working actor.

And my fire has never gone out.

Chapter 38

THE BEST YEARS

"To love what you do and feel that it matters,
how could anything be more fun?"

– Katherine Graham

By Patty Zenizo & Nancy Irwin

M Y CONTRACTED JOB OF eight years had finally ended. The economy was tough at the time, and everyone I knew was working two jobs just to make their former salary! So I thought, why not start my own business? After all, I reasoned, if it didn't work out, I would go out and find other work.

Luckily, I didn't have to look very far for inspiration—my former boss and my main vendor had each started their own businesses while in their 40s. They were the perfect examples to follow, both confident and successful. They also offered me valuable assistance and support.

So at 44, I started a business of my own—an insurance agency, Preferred Bonding & Insurance Services. And it's doing great. My background is in social work, so I feel I use my compassion and understanding for ambitious construction companies that need assistance in their growth and development. My company and I have a very good reputation; in fact, at times, I've been called the Goddess of Bonding because 95% of the time we get the bond for the client; and if we can't get it, it's probably because it can't be done. Preferred Bonding and Insurance Services can pull off miracles in terms of meeting the needs of the client; in our case, building contractors. And we do it with a smile. Our motto is "The difficult we do right away, but the impossible takes a little longer."

Financially, I'm in a position that has allowed me to make good investments and help family members. I have to say my midlife years are proving to be my best! Because of my life and work experiences, I've been able to meet every opportunity and challenge that has come my way. And the best part of all? I was (and am) able to deal with all the success that has come my way, too.

Chapter 39

FIND THE GOAL POSTS AND
KEEP AIMING FOR THEM

"Sometimes there aren't second chances. Sometimes it's now or never."

– Joe Montana

By Matt Armstrong & Nancy Irwin

WORKING WITH TECHNOLOGY WAS never my goal in life. It was just something I grew up with. I was around computers before Bill Gates signed his contract with IBM, because my dad was an early computer programmer. As a kid, I would call the computer on the rotary phone and put the handset into the acoustic couplers on the modem so I could play a game. Real old-school stuff. But the truth was, I always found technology rather boring.

However, it was a quick and easy to make money to pay for school. While I was the treasurer and then president of my fraternity and going to school, I was supporting myself as a programmer and computer consultant. My original plan was to study German and Russian and go to Czechoslovakia in 1991-92 to help the new capitalists get on their feet following the collapse of the Berlin Wall. I went as far as talking to the State Department about permits for me and my computer (then classified as a munition!) for working in Prague.

However, one summer, when I was supposed to be working and making money, I spent all of my time taking care of issues at my fraternity. Unfortunately, no income meant no college, so I left school. I supported myself by staying on the technology route, which meant, of course, putting my dreams on hold.

Years later, I became a "technologist" for a large mutual fund company where I designed, developed and managed a variety of systems, including a fun one that kept the company in compliance with SEC and foreign equivalents of the SEC. One of my last projects was architecting, building and managing a system that captured hundreds of thousands of paper documents and turned them into electronic documents for global access, disaster recovery and compliance conformance.

After a dozen years in the knowledge management field, I was really bored with computers, technology and the path that I found myself on. My work had become a way of funding my lifestyle outside of work, mainly training for Ironman distance triathlons. I knew I could do more than just punching a clock.

In my late 30s, I knew that my life and my ambitions needed a detour. I no longer wanted to continue traveling this safe yet unchallenging and tedious route that was unfulfilling. Boredom with work is probably what led me in the first place to racing in five Ironman triathlons, dozens of marathons, a few ultra-marathons (nearly every weekend had a 100-mile training bike ride, a 3-mile ocean swim and at least 10 miles of running). Perhaps it was my own special midlife crisis. I believed then as I do now that life is too short to simply clock in and out of life. You should enjoy what you do. Clearly it was time for a change and time to return to what I always wanted to do: playing a part in international relations and national security issues. I wanted to make a difference in the world and my current position wasn't the right platform to do it.

My wife has always been my No. 1 supporter, so we sat down together and discussed what was really important to us and what I wanted to do with the second half of my life.

I had done pretty well financially and professionally, considering I didn't have a college degree, but the plans and dreams that I made in college still lived inside me. I thought, "Why not pick up where I left off, return to college and finish my undergraduate degree in international relations—and maybe get a graduate degree afterward?"

With a plan in place, I stayed at my job while I prepared for the switch. By the time I left, I anticipated an easy transition. Wrong. It was an extremely difficult one.

But there were the constant nagging fears and questions: "What am I doing? How many tricks can you teach an old dog? How radical is this? Can I really contribute to the discussion?" I asked myself, "Who will hire me?" Not because I'm an old guy, but because I couldn't afford to start at the bottom in an internship or a $20,000–a-year job ... not without negatively impacting my family's standard of living. "Was this really a smart decision? Am I really going to get somewhere with this?" I started second-guessing myself, realizing I hadn't completely thought this through.

Then there was the work: old-fashioned schoolwork. After years of writing computer programs, PowerPoint presentations and technical white papers, I had to write formal arguments and cite sources in essay format, and that was tough!

There was also the time factor. I was finishing my undergraduate program in my late 30s, sitting with 19-year-olds who would complain about "not having enough time." Time! What did they know about time?! I had a life—a grown-up's life. In addition to attending school, I worked part-time: I was an endurance athlete and coach with my own clients, including the UCLA triathlon team and the UCLA masters swim team. On top of that, I had a wife and we'd just had our first baby.

But I didn't let any of these concerns deter me or distract me. It took me about 18 months to turn my thinking around and to get over my self-doubt and the negative beliefs. My wife had faith in me, even if I was wondering what I was doing. My professors and the executive director of my graduate program distanced themselves from my work and topic areas because it didn't conform to their world views, but my published work and my blog were increasingly used as a reference by the government, the military and think tanks involved in counterinsurgency and the future of warfare. My self-confidence grew as I received more invitations to author more papers, as well as to present or attend workshops and conferences in the defense community.

Because I got so little support from my academic program, I was and am more aggressive in getting my ideas out there, so I'm actually thankful. In an industry where ideas are currency, I use my blog to insert my unique perspective into the conversation. My blog, more than my academic program, has opened doors. It has resulted in very interesting connections that help me hit the ground running faster than the average graduate student to make the most of my time learning. It's frequently assumed I am doing post-doctoral work. Little do they know I'm completely independent without any advisers—save my informal network of colleagues developed online through the blog.

I returned to school to complete my bachelor's in international relations and now I've just completed my master's in public diplomacy, but not before our second child was born.

While I do not yet have a job lined up, numerous people whom I respect, as well as groups that I want to work with, speak highly of my work and are helping me get the right job.

Although I've taken a circuitous route to get where I am today, I wouldn't have changed anything in the last 20 years. I have no regrets. I'm on the right career path now and very happy with the choices I've made.

As long as I stay on the course I've set for myself, everything will fall into place.

Chapter 40

LOVE IS OUR SPIRITUAL GLUE

"There are two things we need to survive and thrive as human beings: we must know, trust and believe that we are loved and lovable!"

– Dr. Fran

By Frances M. Pastoria, PsyD, & Nancy Irwin, PsyD

"WHO AM I?" "WHY am I here?" "What is the true purpose of my life?" For millennia, humankind has asked those same three questions. We continue to ask those questions today because many of us are living lives of quiet desperation, living with a spiritual disconnect even though we are surrounded by material possessions, good friends, co-workers and strong family relationships. This disconnect, coming from within ourselves, has created feelings of emptiness and loneliness that nothing in our external world is able to fill.

There was a time when I felt those feelings too; a sense of longing that permeated my soul. I was at a loss as to the cause or how to rid myself of it. I was a traditional homemaker with a loving family and beautiful house in the suburbs, and was regarded as a highly respected community leader. Yet with each new accomplishment I found myself asking those same three questions: Who am I? Why am I here? And what is the true purpose of my life?

Then at age 47, I had a phenomenal spiritual experience that connected me to a loving source I found to be so powerful that the connection transformed my thinking in ways that allowed me to see the world as it truly was and not as I believed it to be. Everywhere I looked I saw signs of the love that came from this powerful source. In time I came to realize that I belonged to and was part of a Universal Source Of Light Energy that is so powerful, it can change the darkness of ignorance into the light of understanding ourselves and each other.

The answers to my three questions became crystal clear. Who am I? I am a spiritual being living a lifetime in human form. I am energy in motion. Why am I here? I am here to learn how to integrate my spirituality into my everyday life. My life purpose is to learn how to love and be loved until that process comes as naturally to me as breathing. Love is our spiritual glue. It is what holds us together when all else appears to be falling apart.

I understood that when we allow ourselves to be internally directed we can use our spiritual energy to create, along with our Universal Source, the life that we are truly meant to live. The clearer I understood these things about myself the fuller my life became.

This may sound as if my transformational process ran smoothly and without doubt or fear, but changing myself from the inside-out was, in the beginning, scary business. The strongest fear I had was that I might lose who I believed I was. But I was determined from the very beginning not to let go of anything that was of real importance to me, which was mainly who I believed I was and the important role my family played in my life. My family was my life. In fact, before my spiritual awakening I believed that my family defined who I was. I saw myself as a part of everyone who was important in my life—my parents, my husband and mostly my children. I believed I was a daughter, a sister, a wife and a mother. I believed I could not be happy unless they were all happy. Of course it was an impossible task. The minute one person was happy, someone else was unhappy. With that faulty belief in mind, I became the ultimate caretaker. It took time before I understood the pain and suffering that belief was causing me. My family was a huge, wonderful driving force in my life, but it wasn't until I came to understand that there was a "me" in my life that my life started to change. I was surprised to discover I could be loved just because I was me. That I didn't have to do anything to make them love me. Just being me was enough!

I learned to trust myself and what I believed to be true. I spoke constantly of love because I saw it everywhere. Yet it surprised me that the thought of seeking love in one's life seemed to frighten people. At one point during my transformational process, my husband said to me, "What if you are going crazy but you are convincing me that you are sane?" I told him to watch my behavior; if my life kept getting better then he would know I was not crazy and that through an act of grace, my life was being blessed in some special way." I loved his response. He said, "Honey, I can't say that I believe in most of the things you tell me, like we are spiritual beings here to enlighten the world with our love for instance, but I do believe in you. I will support you the best I can but the rest of what you need you will have to get for yourself." I told him that I appreciated his faith in me, and with the help of the Ancient Voice that has guided me from the beginning of my transformational change—the voice I call the "Woman of the Ages" because she sounds so old and wise—that was exactly what I intended to do.

Even though I had begun to believe in myself, I was not prepared for the changes that would take place in my life. As my beliefs changed, my actions changed and as my actions changed my life experiences changed; they grew deeper in both meaning and purpose.

My life began to unfold in ways I would never have imagined. Upon my husband's retirement, I convinced him that we needed to move from Michigan to California, the land of my dreams. After a few years of easy living, I started college at 60 years of age when most of our friends were retiring and simplifying their lives. During the next six years I earned a bachelor's degree in human behavior psychology, a master's degree in counseling psychology and a doctorate in clinical psychology. To become a doctor of psychology was beyond even my wildest dreams! I have written books and give workshops based on what I have learned from my personal transformational process. I continue to have warm, loving relationships with my family, friends and clients. I am getting better and better at allowing myself to be loved for who I am and being lovable because I love my life.

I think my husband would agree, now that some 30 years have passed, that I am not going crazy and that my life has become richer, more joyful and totally fulfilling. I know for sure that once we place our trust in who we truly are internally and allow ourselves to let go of the limits we place on ourselves externally because we believe we are only who we see in the mirror, we begin the process of transformation by drawing out the potential that lies within each of us. There is within each of us a tiny inner voice longing to be heard. It wants to tell you that if you are willing to listen, it will help you become more than you ever dreamed you could be. I believe that this spiritual potential is not just for some of us but for each and every one of us.

How can we embody all of who and what we are meant to be? What I believe is that if there is love everywhere and in every situation, then what we much teach ourselves to do is look for it. What I teach in my workshops is this: Ask yourself what you believe to be the most loving thing you can do no matter what the situation. Sometimes the most loving thing to do will be to take care of your needs, and sometimes the most loving thing to do will be to take care of the needs of someone else. After you have acted on what you have decided, pay attention to how you feel. All feelings are real. If you feel more loving toward yourself, whether what you decided was in your best interest or someone else's, then you made the right decision. If you feel bad about yourself, then you need to rethink the situation to see if there were other options you might have considered, and vow to make a more conscious choice the next time. The more we work at understanding ourselves and each other, the more enlightened we become. Enlightenment in any form lets us know that our internal connection with our Universal Source Of Light Energy, higher power or whatever name one gives to a power greater than we are, is strong and effective.

We were not created to live lives of quiet desperation. We were created to live lives rich in life experiences, filled with love and understanding of ourselves and each other. A life of fulfillment can only be lived from the inside-out; by staying focused on the internal part of ourselves, which is where we are all the same rather than focusing on the external, where we are constantly dealing with our differences. Believe that you can create a life you are willing to live. Act on that belief and your life could become more than you ever dreamed possible. Mine did, and if it could happen to a middle-age homemaker from a small city in Michigan, it can happen to you too. Remember, love is the answer. Practice how to be loving and believe that you are lovable until it comes to you as easily as breathing. You have the power to create a life that will take you beyond your wildest dreams.

Chapter 41

THE SOUND OF SUCCESS

"The only sure things in life are death and taxes."
– Benjamin Franklin

By Steve Palmer & Nancy Irwin

DON'T KNOW HOW much money I'm going to make this month. I have no idea. It could be $4,000. It could be $10,000. I really don't have a clue and that's scary. The bills come in regardless of my income, and when I don't know what my income is month to month, it can be downright scary.

That's what happens when you're in business for yourself.

After I married, I decided to switch careers. I closed my chain of retail stores in Atlanta and relocated to Chicago, where I began working as a sales representative for a large music distributor, selling their CDs to retail stores like Borders. In the music business, a distributor will represent a number of different labels, and I represented about 200.

When the company went out of business, I decided to take on the clients myself. A lot of companies I worked with didn't have representation, so I just started cold calling, and after a while I was doing pretty well as an independent. A little success fueled my motivation to keep going. Soon, I started signing more and more clients. Now I have a broad spectrum of product and I represent classic, rap, jazz, folk, blues, country, Celtic, heavy metal, cabaret, you name it.

In sales, you always have fears of losing accounts and losing companies that you represent; I've lost some, some have gone out of business and some have changed their business plans so they don't use sales reps anymore. And I'm not making as much as I did five or six years ago because nowadays people are downloading a lot of music from the internet.

That may sound scary, but starting my retail business in Atlanta was far scarier—I had to write up a business plan. I had present it to a bank representative so I could get a loan. I had to get investors and do a lot of things to get that business off the ground. But I was never really scared, or even unsure, about becoming an independent sales rep. I just decided that it was something that I was going to do and I just plowed ahead. I never doubted that it would work if I did it right—and I made sure that I did.

But I'm an optimist. In sales, you have to be an optimist and have faith and trust that your skills and abilities will provide an income.

Anyone with drive, determination and perseverance can succeed. Sure, that's easier said than done, but if you take action, set goals and meet challenges, then you'll come out on top. There's no sweeter music than success and knowing that you've done your best.

I've actually made three major you-turns in middle age. At the age of 39, I got married for the first time. I had lived alone for 15 years and it was a pretty dramatic change to be with someone 24/7. And about 14 months after we got married, our first child was born. So at age 40,

I was a father. Another huge change. But I'll tell you, I've had the most fun ever with my daughter (now 17) and my son (now 14). Some would say having children at 40 and 43 is pushing the envelope. I would say that I probably don't have the energy that I did at age 25, but there is no doubt in my mind that I appreciate the kids more than I would have at that age. I (and my wife, too—we're the same age) had many years to do just what I wanted and had very little responsibility other than to myself. I was very ready to be a father.

Dealing with three big life changes at age 40 was a challenge—but I wouldn't have had it any other way!

Chapter 42

CLICK!

---

*"If you do follow your bliss, you put yourself on a kind of track
that has been there all along, waiting for you, and the life that you
ought to be living is the one you are living. 1 say, follow your bliss, and
doors will open where you didn't know they were going to be."*

– Joseph Campbell

By Molly Brandenburg

EVER EXPERIENCE A "CLICK" moment? It's a sudden, overwhelming feeling that some sort of change is coming. Some people may call it self-realization or an epiphany, but I call it a "click," like the sound of something being turned on—or off.

I've always been attuned to my innermost senses, but somewhere in my adult years, circumstances dulled my senses and I lost the ability to feel or to see what was staring me in my face. I no longer felt aware of much of anything. I could no longer hear the "click."

I began my career working in the Warner Bros. office of Frank Sinatra, answering letters and taking care of personal business for "the chairman of the board." I then worked as a copywriter for advertising agencies, movie studios and in corporate communications. At the same time I was developing my "corporate" career, I also pursued a career in theater. I performed in nightclubs as "Miss Peggy Judy," a comedic lounge singer character I'd developed in improvisation workshops and shows.

I performed evenings and weekends, and toured throughout California. It provided an important outlet and kept me going creatively while I put in long hours at the office. At lunch time, I would hole up in a coffee shop and work on ideas for a cartoon book.

Sounds fun, huh? At times it was, but as humans, we only have so much time and so much energy to go around. Through the years, as I tried to juggle my dream career with my corporate life, I became exhausted. Every job took a little piece of me, and my relationship with my husband slowly deteriorated.

I wanted to leave the corporate world and do creative work full-time, but in my exhaustion, I couldn't see a way to make any sort of real change. Finally, I fell into despair and my health suffered. I felt incapable of making any sort of change.

When my father was diagnosed with Alzheimer's, I, along with my mother and brothers, endured the agony of watching our dad, who had been a highly successful doctor and passionate artist, slip little by little into what doctors call the "long goodbye."

Then one day, as I sat with my father in the Alzheimer's nursing home—with my own little girl playing happily on the floor in his room—I suddenly realized with clarity how short our active time in life really is, and how much of my life was unsatisfactory.

I held Dad's hand. He patted my leg affectionately, as he always had. Though he was no longer able to speak coherently, we still shared a strong bond. I felt that, if he could speak, he would say, "Molly, you must use your time. Don't let it slip away. Now, now is your time. Don't wait any longer to really achieve the life you want. If you want to change your life, you need to do it now."

Click. Even before his death, I had felt something inside me changing. Tectonic plates were moving beneath my feet, even if I wasn't consciously aware of them. I had to face what was obvious—I could no longer muster up any sort of enthusiasm for the life I was living. I realized that, as my dad had shown me, my chance to really achieve what I wanted in life was limited. I had tried so hard to be a "good girl"—out of a misguided sense of loyalty to others. I had invested in trying to be who others wanted me to be instead of being true to myself.

Big questions surfaced. Why was the only obstacle facing me, me? Why had I neglected my creative and spiritual gifts, only to play the role of the person I thought others wanted me to be? Why had I spent my life serving others to the point of dangerously devaluing myself?

Somewhere along the line I had stopped loving me. The life I was living—while it offered financial security and structure—was severely limiting. I had given up my hopes and dreams to fulfill everyone else's. It was a painful revelation, but nevertheless...somewhere in my despair ... my senses came alive again. A switch turned on that turned my black and white world into one that glowed with luminous color.

I began to see that the change had really started years before. When I was laid off from my job at the movie studio, I'd actually thought, "Good. Bring it on!" I knew it was a step toward reclaiming myself. And after the birth of my daughter, I made the decision not to go back to a full-time corporate job but to freelance and stay home with my baby. Unfortunately, that caused even more stress within my little family.

The stresses had mounted, as my father's illness took a toll on our entire family. Finally I summoned up the courage to face my unhappiness, and after 17 years of marriage, I filed for divorce. I had fears, of course—fears of social disapproval and the loss of financial stability. But I couldn't turn back. So I kept moving forward.

My father died. My divorce was finalized. I moved out of the house where I'd lived for 18 years. At the age of 45, it was time to start over.

I gave myself time to regroup and then opened up the cartoon book I'd been working on while my daughter was in preschool. It was time to take another look. I picked up my drawing pencil and started on one more revision of the book I'd worked on for years, about the playful activities of my cats, Seymour and Frankie.

I sent it out. One editor really liked it, but her company turned it down. I sent it to another publisher, and they turned it down. It was a "click" moment. As I held the rejected manuscript in my hand, I decided to publish it myself. I'd been through too much to go through years of submissions and rejection letters. I wanted to just get it out in front of people and see how it fared.

I published it online with a "print on demand" e-publisher and sold it out of the trunk of my car and on Amazon.com over Christmas. Its enthusiastic reception persuaded me to take it to the New York Book Expo in June 2007. I bought a booth and had an eye-catching poster made of the cat cartoons. The book was quickly noticed by the buyers from Barnes & Noble, who submitted it to a publisher for me.

Two months after the show, I had an offer from Sterling Publishing to buy my original book, "Everyday Cat Excuses: Why I Can't Do What You Want."

CLICK! CLICK! CLICK! I looked up and was sure I saw my dad up in heaven, smiling back down at me.

Like many of us, I got caught up in the moments of my everyday life and lost sight of myself. It was a scary, desperate place to be. But it taught me a lot. You *can* change your life. If you are afraid, seek out family, friends or a church for support. And you can find support in books. There are many spiritually oriented books available. I recommend *Excuse Me, Your Life is Waiting*, a book that emphasizes positive energy in the midst of life challenges.

My experience has taught me that it's worth it to take the chance of truly, truly opening your heart to change, of having the courage to truly be yourself and to honor your gifts. It's amazing who and what can walk into your life to help and support you if you really open your heart. Tell God you are ready for anything. Stop judging. Stop trying to control. Just let things be, and see what happens. Always love yourself first and foremost.

And one other thing I learned: divorced parents can remain friends and be partners in caring for their children in a healthy relationship, if they really really work at it. Counseling and support are critical to surviving a divorce with a child's well being intact.

Here's a quote I love from an anonymous writer: "It's good to be alive, and to have been alive, for whatever length of time, in this beautiful world."

Life is precious, and far too short. It's worth it to live the life you were meant to live.

Chapter 43

FIND YOUR PASSION AND LIVE IT

"1 never met a man 1 didn't like"

– Will Rogers

By Myke Michaels & Nancy Irwin

JIMI HENDRIX SANG, "THERE must be some way out of here." Well, there is always a way out—you just have to find it. If someone lends you a hand, hold it. If you see a door, open it. If you come across a different path, take it. If there's one thing I've learned, it's that it's all up to *you*. You can blame your parents, blame the schools, blame society, but you know what? It's all up to you.

Because I was born in 1954, I guess I'm called a baby boomer ... but I didn't have the remodeled basement, BBQ grill in the back yard, "hey guys, come over and watch The Mickey Mouse Club" kind of life or the Donna Reed kind of mom in high heels and pearls who would greet us kids with milk and cookies when we came home from school. Those images may have sold a lot of *Life* magazines back then, but it had nothing to do with me or my neighborhood.

I grew up in a strange and physically abusive home in the gang-infested streets of South Central Los Angeles. There are many loving families there; mine just wasn't one of them.

Growing up like I did, where I did, I had to physically fight to survive. I wouldn't say I was in any gangs—and a lot of kids in South Central aren't—but I've always been a fighter: street fighter, semi-pro boxer, martial artist … and I still carry the physical scars. I was 12 years old the first time I was stabbed. I was trying to help a friend who'd gotten jumped. Actually, that's happened a few times. I'm fiercely loyal to my friends, and if I think that someone's getting hurt, I'm there; I don't even think about it. Over the next few years I got shot or stabbed about five times.

My parents split when I was 8 years old. I lived with my mom until I was 10, and then my dad got custody. Even though I was leaving an abusive situation, I never felt like my dad was rescuing me. He was married to the most evil and mentally abusive woman I have ever known before or since. Even my dad wondered about her. I wanted to be left alone; basically, I'd raised myself. Why did I need a parent? I never felt like I ever needed anybody—I'd always taken care of myself. Don't get me wrong, I love people in my life but I never had that "Oh, my God, I'm scared of being alone" feeling. I love life, I appreciate it, but my nickname is "The Wolf," and a wolf can be happy in a pack or off by himself.

I got good grades in school, but it never occurred to me to play it smart. I got in trouble there, at home, and eventually I got together with some other guys and broke into people's houses. But something turned me around—I got caught. And it was the best thing to happen to me. Later convicted of 26 counts of burglary and two counts of armed robbery, I learned that when you're going to jail, you only have two choices—repeat your mistake, or don't. And I don't like repeating myself. I needed a quick exit out of Los Angeles, and when I was given the choice of jail or the military, I joined the Navy. I became a field medic attached to a S.E.A.L. team. I was then shipped to the Philippines and then on to Vietnam, where my job was to tag and bag soldiers' bodies to be shipped back home so their families could properly bury them.

At the end of 1971, I got a request from an officer who was friends with me, and was recruited into a special U.S. task force; it's not the CIA or FBI, but a special unit set up by the U.S. government to hunt for people wanted by the law for a variety of offenses. I was only 18 years old. After almost a year of training, I traveled the world in a variety of short-term cover jobs, doing what I had to do before leaving the task force after four years. I was like a mercenary hired by the government to take out the trash, but I had to locate the trash first. The job was offered to me for a four-year term, so when I was up for renewal, I felt I was done doing what others thought was right for me.

Then I made another transition. Since I had some medical training, I studied and became an inhalation therapist, but three weeks into my first job, a young boy died in the ER. I knew this wasn't for me.

So I became a bouncer, taught martial arts, started getting into stunts, worked as a bounty hunter and even tried performing comedy at clubs around LA. Then in 1985, a friend asked, "Hey, you want to go to a hair show? It's a great way to pick up women." Imagining that a hair show was like some sort of nightclub, I said, "Sure." But when I got there, I saw the art that was involved in it. Yeah, I know what you're thinking—art? But like any art form, it's taking something that was nothing and turning it into something beautiful.

Once again, at age 36, I went into a different direction. I studied hair and makeup, and I'm not talking lip liner. I studied special effects makeup, too, and got to work on TV shows like *Babylon 5*, the TV movie *She Creature: The Mermaid Chronicles* and many others. I quickly moved to the top of the ladder, and now I have a long list of movie, TV, advertising and music video credits. I've been nominated for a few Emmys and I've won a couple; I've been part of the teams nominated for an Oscar® for both *Master and Commander* with Russell Crowe as well as for *Time Machine* with Guy Pearce.

I enjoy what I do now and I have a great time. I wouldn't change anything.

I've probably had 10 different careers, but only one definition of success and one definition of life: *passion*. You have to have passion in everything you do. No matter what it is, if you don't have passion for what you're doing, why are you doing it? There are so many people sitting behind desks or digging ditches or hanging clothes on a rack who hate their jobs. But they're doing it, why? I'd rather be doing something I love for $50 a day than something I hate for $1,000 a day. You have to enjoy what you do, and if you don't, you can't possibly do it the way it should be done. If that's the case, step aside and let somebody else do it.

I've always changed careers, not because I was bored with them, but because I fell in love with my new one. Having passion leaves you open to new experiences, new opportunities, new adventures and new business and artistic ventures.

Now I'm ready to make a transition into acting and producing. I've formed my own production company, Wolf Pack Film Works, and started looking at scripts. And a production company is like any business—there are plans to be made and goals to set up.

Through all my many career choices I've learned that to get what you want, you have to know what you want. You can't just dream and wish that what you want will come to you. Set up a plan, a timeline; expect failure and push through the fear. Fear is a state of mind anyway, not a reality. Fear may be normal, but don't let it keep you from doing what you want. Do you really want to be sitting there at age 60, full of regrets for things you didn't do? Plans you didn't make? Opportunities you didn't take?

Finally, respect yourself for even thinking about making a change. Because if you don't respect yourself, nobody else will. For me, getting from point A to point B and every point in between has been a long, twisted, mangled road full of potholes, and many times

I had to build my own exits, but I have no regrets for the successes and failures that I've created and the passion that I still hold for the future.

DR. IRWIN'S SELF-HELP TIPS FOR VEERING OFF ON YOUR OWN:

1. The word motivation comes from the Latin "to move." Self-motivators start their own motors. The mistake many make is to wait until they feel motivated before they act. That's like waiting for your car to start itself before you drive it. YOU make your motivation. Certainly, fear can be a great motivator, but that generally is an external force. You can poke a hole in that phantom fear by motivating yourself.

2. Break your process down to simple steps and figure out just what putting the key in the ignition would be.

3. Create a mission statement for yourself: What is the point of your goal? How will it serve humanity?

4. From that mission statement, it should be easy to know what your values are. The mission is the purpose of the trip: the values are the wheels that get you there.

5. Write out your short-term goals. Your mission is the big picture; now plan the short-terms goals that keep you moving toward your destination.

6. Check in with yourself periodically. Reward or at least acknowledge yourself for how far you've come. Honor ALL progress, no matter how slow it seems. Remember, we get whatever we focus on, and if you focus on how slow or behind you are, you'll only create more of the same.

7. The actress and great wit Carrie Fisher says, "If my life weren't funny, it'd be true." This is a woman who has been diagnosed with a serious mental illness—bipolar disorder. She continually finds a way to turn pain into humor. Can you use humor and laughter to get a new perspective on your situation?

8. Celebrate all milestones and wins along the way.

9. Share your success and your road stories with others. Remember where you started … that is your unique path. No one else's is quite the same.

10. Set new goals. It is human nature to always yearn for something, even if it is simply rest and reflection. Many people who find success very young end up tanking because they don't know how to set new goals. They imagined their goal was the end of the road. Success is always a starting point. Great people keep expanding.

"Why not go out on a limb? Isn't that where the fruit is?"
Mark Twain

DR. IRWIN'S SELF-HELP TIPS FOR DRIVING YOUR BUSINESS ON A SHOESTRING BUDGET

1. Most communities have a Small Business Development Center that offers FREE counseling for start-up businesses. With an on-staff attorney, website/e-commerce technologist, banker/funding specialist and accountant/QuickBooks instructor, they offer no-cost counseling. Click on http://lbsbdc.lbcc.edu/consultants.htm to take advantage of this information in Southern California, or call (562) 570–4574 for a local referral.

2. SCORE (Southern California Organization of Retired Executives) also offers free advice for a diversity of businesses. You can Google them in your area and get free advice via email or telephone. Get into high gear with the help of retired successful businessmen and women to grow your business.

3. Every city has Rotary, Kiwanis, Optimists, Elks and Lions Clubs, as well as Chambers of Commerce. These are very cost-effective ways of networking. Also, these clubs need a regular speaker for their luncheons or breakfasts. You can bill yourself as a speaker to spread awareness about your business. You'll get a free meal and a coffee mug!

4. There are a host of other networking organizations, whose fees vary. Le Tip and BNI (Business Networking International) are two of the most popular groups of this nature, but Google your town or city and find similar organizations.

5. Not happy with these? Start your own! Find a local diner or steakhouse with a private room and tack up flyers, get on the phone and start talking up your own group.

6. Post an advertisement Craig's List. Also on You Tube and My Space. These are 100% free and get thousands of clicks daily. Of course, ezines are free as well. Continually update your contact list, and you can save thousands of dollars by direct mail. When you have the capital, get your own website and have it search-engine optimized.

That is now becoming as important as a business card. You can make money while you sleep!

7. Consider making a presentation to a PTA, church, synagogue or even local singles events, if your product or service is pertinent. Never underestimate the power of grassroots networking. Word of mouth is a powerful medium.

8. Many local businesses have community bulletin boards—grocery stores, bagel shops, coffee houses, etc. You can make a slick color flyer and post that with business cards. Keep checking back intermittently to replenish.

9. You can earn money by sitting in traffic: consider a bumper sticker, a magnetic sign, and/or a vanity license plate (with contact info on the frame). Watching drivers in your rearview mirror read your bumper is a great way to offset road rage, too!

10. You can go to a local trophy shop and have a nameplate badge made up with your name, business name, and/or profession. Wear this at all times when you are dressed professionally, and you'll be surprised how you pick up clients. You can turn waiting in line at the market or the car wash into a business relationship. Remember that EVERYTHING is networking!

11. Find a mentor. Most successful people LOVE to talk about their road to success. Invite this person to lunch and tell him or her, frankly, you'd like to be him/her when you grow up. They can give you invaluable advice, shortcuts, help, maybe even financial backing.

12. If you are a service business, you can start a business with very little cash. I started my private practice with $3,000. $1,500 for the office space lease (including deposit and first and last month's rent), $500 for a beautiful desk/credenza set from a used-office-furniture store, and $1,000 for a computer and a phone. By using the tips above, my practice grew. Don't forget about swap meets and flea markets, the ole barter system, the Salvation Army and other thrift stores, estate sales and used-appliance stores to build your office on a budget. I

found this a very fun and creative part of the process. It was like playing house when I was a little girl!

13. Equally creative is your vision. You get to design your business (and your life) as you wish. Write a business plan. You can download a template from the internet. Or take an extension course or a business 101 course from a local community college, or an online distance learning course. Make some decisions: How much money do you want to make in your first year? First quarter? How many clients/widgets do you need to make that goal? What does it take to create one client/widget?

14. Try a little self-hypnosis. Close your eyes and just imagine your office/studio/store. Where is it? What does it look like? What do you hear? Smell? Feel? What do the clients/patients/patrons look like? What is their profile?

15. Make a list of every single thing you will need, from paper clips to $100K loan. Believe me, after a while it becomes as easy to manifest the $100K as it does the paper clips. They all simply become things to do on your things to do list. As author Napoleon Hill says: "Reduce your plan to writing. The moment you complete this, you will have definitely given concrete form to the intangible desire."

16. If you are a product business, or a service business that requires substantial equipment, and you are not a millionaire, consider a business loan. This country is built on the small-business person, so check with your bank and local small-business development organization to get the seed money you need. If you are ethnic or female, check into business loans, foundations, and grants that support these individuals. Make sure you have a very well-written, powerful mission statement to sell your idea, as well as a tight business plan.

17. Use your own creativity and ingenuity. Think outside the box. There are many paths to success, and you can find your own.

18. Unplug from the statistics, the "they say," "what if" and "yeah, but" voices. Life is built on exceptions. Be an exception!

"A ship in harbor is safe. But that is not what ships are for."
John A. Shedd

ACKNOWLEDGEMENTS

I am so blessed to have such an amazing support system in my life. Thank you for being you!

Melissa Lentz James, editor extraordinaire! Your brilliance is surpassed only by your enthusiasm and commitment to excellence.

Lindsay Hall and Kayla Soper for their graphic designs and ability to spin on a dime!

My core people, my closest friends: Joseph Praner, Mitch Friedman, Karen Lorshbough, Charles Gardner, Suzanna Sahakian, Ann Gunder, Bruce Bailey, Farris Goodrum, Leon Williams, Marc Rudisill, Lucy Jones, Vicki Hillebrand. Each of you has always been there for me with nothing but faith, laughter and loving support. You are my heart!

My colleagues at the clinic: John McGrail, Lisa Percival, Chiyo Maniwa, Gina DeMasi, and Susan Lindau. Thank you for all your support and brilliance. You make me proud.

Dr. Leslie Nichols, a wonderful therapist who gave me tools to change when I didn't have a clue.

All my alma maters (I needed a lot of schoolin'!) West Georgia University (Dr. Beheruz N. Sethna and Frank Pritchett in particular), Georgia State University, Southern California University and Hypnosis Motivation Institute.

Children of the Night, for changing my life.

My dear parents, Brigadier General Clarence B. and Florrie Irwin, whose values constantly teach me that some things are best unchanged.

My three beautiful sisters, Susan Grills, Laura Rogers and Mary Spearman.

My brothers-in-law: Terry Rogers (I can't thank you enough for all your loving support in this endeavor), Dennis Grills and Brad Spearman, for having the good sense to marry my sisters.

All the patients who walk through my doors and honor me on their path to healing. You continually inspire me and amaze with your courage to change. You make my you-turn worth it all and more!

ABOUT THE AUTHOR

Originally from Atlanta, where she trained as an opera singer, Dr. Nancy Irwin moved to New York City in 1985 to pursue a career as a stand-up comedian. She worked all over the country and abroad, and moved to L.A. in 1994 when she heard that Hollywood needed more blondes...

Dr. Nancy experienced an epiphany when she began volunteer work for Children of the Night, a shelter for sexually abused children in Los Angeles. It changed her life, and prompted her to pursue a doctorate in psychology and to specialize in the prevention and healing of child sexual abuse.

A pre-licensed psychologist and clinical therapeutic hypnotist, Dr. Nancy is in private practice in Los Angeles, and is also a busy public speaker for Children of the Night, the Rape and Incest National Network, and Planned Parenthood. She's been quoted extensively in *Cosmopolitan, Redbook, Women's World*, and others, and has appeared on numerous radio and TV shows, including The Greg Behrendt Show, The Fashion Network, Blind Date to name a few. Dr. Irwin is a member of the American Academy of Experts in Traumatic Stress, a member of the Southern California Society of Clinical Hypnosis, and sits on the Education Committee of the California Coalition on Sexual Offending.

You-Turn is her first book.

www.makeayou-turn.com
www.drnancyirwin.com